I0789744

Harold Washington
and the
Civil Rights Legacy

Second edition

Christopher Chandler

Woodbury Press

Second Edition: September 2017
Printed in the United States of America
ISBN: 978-1976324246
2.1

Contents

Foreword

Harold Washington and the Civil Rights Legacy is a gripping account by Chris Chandler of Washington's historic campaign, his tumultuous time as mayor, the civil rights movement that preceded him, and the transformation which followed. It fills out the story not only of Harold Washington but the ragtag, heroic, and eccentric folks who transformed the movement into a government.

Chris recounts this story as an insider, one of the whites in the rainbow coalition. He is a radical journalist who helped elect Harold but could still be critical of his shortcomings.

Chris concludes that the prophesy in Harold Washington's inaugural address has been fulfilled: He was "the mayor who cared about people...was...fair...and who saw that city renewed." Among his achievements, Harold instituted affirmative action, allowed city employees to unionize, and provided the opportunity for many of his loyalists still to hold positions of power to move forward a progressive agenda thirty years after his death.

As one of the few charismatic orators who could rival Dr. Martin Luther King, Jr., he was able to provide hope for those shut out of power.

Beyond any specific accomplishments, Mayor Washington has become a legendary figure who symbolizes what Chicago can become.

There has been speculation as to what would have happened if Harold had lived and been mayor for the twenty years he anticipated. Certainly, more progressive changes would have been instituted at City Hall in the years of a continuing Washington administration. Yet it is easier to be certain about what did happen because Harold Washington was mayor than about what would have happened had he lived. Former members of his administration make this legitimate claim: the floor has been permanently raised for quality and equality in city government. A black man was elected mayor. We had minority school superintendents and police chiefs and affirmative action in municipal jobs and contracts. And despite black control, the city didn't fall into Lake Michigan as many whites had feared. Minorities can run the city at least as well as whites. Now everybody knows that is true.

Because of Harold Washington, neighborhoods will never again be completely powerless. The old Chicago machines is not "dead, dead, dead" as Harold proclaimed. Patronage of the old sort still survives, but it is on the wane. The Shakman Decree that Washington signed is finally being enforced and the federal court has ruled that we have made enough progress since the Richard M. Daley administration that there no longer has to be an appointed court monitor on hiring at city hall.

In short, Chicago will never be the same. Chicago was permanently changed for the better by Harold Washington. Very few people in our 170-year history have had that effect. His life and his legacy give us hope. Those of us lucky enough to have known him have been touched by a certain magic, a certain steely idealism which is rare. His legacy lives because of that.

Chris Chandler adds to our understanding of the Washington movement and the broader struggle for transformation. He provides us a front row seat from which to see from the inside this pivotal time in our history. The story he tells is of the continuing clash of reformers vs. the machine, discrimination vs. integration, and citizen empowerment vs. boss control. Harold's triumph is to be celebrated as an inspiration for future struggles. Chris Chandler gives us a clear-eyed, honest account unhindered by myths that sometimes cloud our view of this critical era in Chicago history.

Dick Simpson
Professor of Political Science
The University of Illinois at Chicago

Foreword 2

Chicago has been described by political scientists, activists and commentators alike as the epicenter of Black Politics in America. Columbia University Professor Fredrick C. Harris in his book *The Price of the Ticket,* entitled chapter 2 "Chicago: The Political Capital of Black America." All of these descriptions are accurate because they have been documented by political historians and political scientists such as Harold Gosnell, *Negro Politicians: The Rise of Negro Politics in Chicago;* Ira Katznelson, *Black Men, White Cities;* and Christopher R. Reed's seminal works on Chicago, *The Depression Comes to Chicago's South Side: Protest and Politics, 1930-1933* and *The Rise of Chicago's Black Metropolis, 1920-1929.*

These writers carefully describe the phenomenal rise of Black activism in Chicago that led to the election of Blacks to office as far back as 1871 when John Jones was elected to the Cook County Board and in 1929 when Oscar De Priest was elected the first Black to serve in the U. S. Congress from the North.

All of this political activism set a tradition of Black Chicagoans being in the vanguard of big-city northern politics that has lasted to the present. African Americans in the City of Chicago have combined activism and protest with electoral politics and, thus, were able to lead the fight for Civil Rights in the North in the post-WWII era on the issues of open housing and education. In 1955 with the lynching of Black Chicago teenager Emmett Till in Mississippi by white Klansmen, these activists helped launch a national anti-lynching campaign that kicked off the modern Civil Rights Movement of the 1960s. Therefore, it was inevitable that these activists would invite Dr. Martin Luther King, Jr. to the city to highlight their struggle for open housing, better schools and equal rights.

Christopher Chandler, a Harold Washington loyalist who served as his Press Secretary in his 1983 campaign and in his administration, in this book begins by describing the impact of the 1966 King Crusade on the political establishment, namely Mayor Daley and his entrenched political machine. As Chandler documents, the King Crusade and the Chicago activists' followup led to the first major blow to the Daley machine when Daley conceded to the demands for open housing.

It was that political opening that was claimed by a combined group of Black-led political activists and a multiracial coalition of community groups from across the city that laid the groundwork for the eventual election of Harold Washington, the first Black Mayor of the city.

From this historical foundation Chandler takes us on a Press Secretary's first-person description of the trials and victories of the Washington 1983 and 1987 campaigns and inside the Washington Administration's decision-making process. At the death of Mayor Washington in 1987, he describes the decomposition of the Washington coalition and the disastrous Alderman Timothy Evans Campaign for Mayor of 1989, which was the last major attempt of the Washington Coalition to make a comeback.

He details his disappointments in chapter 7, "Later Campaigns" in which he sketches the political activism of Harold's movement to the present day. He shows us how and why we are indebted to Harold Washington the man, and the coalition that he created and led. His last chapter, "Harold's Legacy," describes the powerful impact he has had on Chicago.

Chandler was and remains a dedicated progressive who is a talented writer and campaign strategist. Unsurprisingly, this book demonstrates the political foundation built by Washington and Jesse Jackson, which led to the election of Barack Obama, President of the United States. Lastly, Chandler shows us that no other city in America other than Chicago could have served as the launching pad for the election of the first Black President. We are certain that Harold would have been proud!

Robert T. Starks, Professor Emeritus
The Carruthers Center for Inner City Studies
Northeastern Illinois University

Introduction

The heart of the book describes the time I worked for Harold Washington, Chicago's first black mayor, first as Press Secretary in his 1983 Democratic primary upset victory, then as Deputy Press Secretary for the general election and the first year and a half of "Council Wars." During that time I had a chance to see some of the inner workings of the election campaigns and his battle to gain control of the City Council.

Everyone who lived in Chicago at that time has their own vivid memories of that 1983 primary battle between Mayor Jane Byrne, State's Attorney Richard M. Daley and U.S. Representative Harold Washington, and Harold's upset victory. We remember the bitter racial hatred of the general election contest against Bernard Epton, and the years of gridlock of Council Wars, as Alderman Edward Vrdolyak led 29 aldermen to control the 50 member city council against Washington's 21.

But it is remembered mostly through the eyes of the major media. This book offers the perspective of Washington's press office. In our eyes, starting with the Epton campaign and running through the first year of Council Wars, the media's coverage was mostly biased and sometimes outrageous. Only when Washington began gaining power did the coverage become more balanced.

The first two chapters describe some of the key events that paved the way for Harold's victory, beginning with Dr. Martin Luther King's 1966 Chicago Crusade, the King riots of 1968 and the assassination of Fred Hampton in 1969. Almost all the important players in Washington's primary victory were part of a movement that was deeply affected by Hampton's death.

The next three chapters cover the time I worked for Washington, and the final three chapters deal with Washington's death, the aftermath of his movement, and an assessment of his accomplishments. His effect on Chicago has been profound, and his movement has the potential to rise again.

Washington was a man who had spent his entire life within the Democratic Party, and from the very beginning he was intent on bringing about justice for the black community by working within the party. When he died of a heart attack in 1987 he had obtained his highest dreams. He had been elected to a second term. He had taken over control of the Cook County Democratic Party. He was emerging as a major opponent to President Ronald Reagan's agenda. He left behind a political legacy of a true rainbow coalition, demanding equity for all parts of the city. That legacy lives on, in the Bernie Sanders movement and in the future of the progressive wing of the Democratic Party.

Chapter 1

Dr. Martin Luther King's 1966 Chicago Crusade

Long thought to be a failure, it was his last victory.

Dr. Martin Luther King announced his "Northern Crusade" in Chicago in January, 1966. The civil rights movement had won important victories for public accommodations and voting rights in the South. Now Dr. King was going to tackle the Northern versions of discrimination. He announced the launching of the Chicago campaign, to be called the Chicago Freedom Movement, a partnership between his Southern Christian Leadership Conference and Chicago's major civil rights group, the Coordinating Council of Community Organizations.

I covered his press conference for the Sun-Times, and wrote how the campaign would begin by bringing people to an understanding of the "internal colonialism" of the slums, which he compared to the exploitation of African colonies. He said he would be living part-time in a West Side tenement while working to organize black high school students, street gangs and the unemployed.

I was struck by how radical his plans were, calling for empowering the powerless. The Chicago civil rights movement had been focused on school segregation and the racial policies of schools superintendent Ben Willis. Dr. King was talking about changing the nature of the city.

He said they would build three kinds of organizations: unions of slum dwellers to engage in collective bargaining with their landlords; Operation Breadbasket, to negotiate for more jobs for blacks and back up negotiations with boycotts; and an "Action Unit of the Unemployed," which would be trained in the discipline of non-violence. He also called for establishing a citizen's review board to investigate changes of police misconduct.

King said he hoped to "disseminate the philosophy of non-violence and find creative ways of grappling with the evils of the northern ghetto."[1]

My wife Marthe and I were living at 1368 N. Sedgwick, in the Old Town Gardens apartments. We saw that Dr. King was proposing tenants unions, so we went to a meeting of the Tenants Advisory Council, and met a number of fellow residents who were committed to civil rights and concerned about what was being done to the complex. We learned that the owners were "turning it over" by advertising only in the black press, charging higher rents and cutting clean up staff.

We developed the slogan "Raise the rents, lower the services, blame the Negroes." We renamed the organization "Tenants Action Council," and David McCullough became our leader. He lived in our building with his mother and younger brother, who was half black. David became so

---

[1] *Chicago Sun-Times*, January 1966.

involved that he took a leave of absence from his job as an electrical engineer to devote full time to the cause.

We held weekly meetings where every tenant could speak and vote. We elected new officers and started picketing the manager's office, demanding to negotiate. McCullough found out that the manager, Sam Lane, was a slum landlord, extracting rents from several rat-infested West Side apartment buildings. He led a tour of one of the slums in East Garfield Park. There were rat holes and peeling paint and rotting stairs. A number of our tenants, including my wife Marthe, developed a deep commitment to fighting this kind of injustice.

I asked Lane for an interview. He suggested we have supper at an Old Town restaurant. Over dessert he went into a tirade about black tenants, and tenants in general. I excused myself, went to the men's room and wrote down his exact words.

The next day I wrote up the story, quoting TAC leaders and Lane. The copy desk brought up the concern that I was a tenant. The city editor, Jim Hoge, decided to run the story but remove my by-line. (I later realized we had mishandled that story. At the least there should have been full disclosure that I had written the story and was a tenant.)

Our tenants union held new elections for officers, building representatives and stairwell reps. We had guest speakers like Al Raby, the head of the Coordinating Council of Community Organizations (the CCCO), and Jesse Jackson, a new young aide to Dr. King. Especially helpful were union organizers sent by the Freedom Movement like

Milton Cohen. A veteran of the Spanish Civil War, he became our most trusted adviser. My wife and I were members of the steering committee, which met almost every night as the campaign intensified.

We started off thinking we should have a "model lease" which would give tenants more rights. Then we joined the movement's drive for the bargaining rights of a union. By July we had decided we should become a cooperative. We tenants should own the building and run our own community. We were white and black, young and old, well off and poor. We would celebrate integration and diversity. We would have a credit union, and promote new tenant-owned enterprises.

McCullough was beginning to work with tenant leaders at Cabrini Green, the giant public housing project a few blocks south. They too should own their own buildings, and have rooftop gardens and restaurants with a view of Lake Michigan. Why not fishing fleets, since they bordered the Chicago River? I was to pursue that dream for public housing for decades to come.

Many of us socialized at the Sacred Cow across the street on Sedgwick, a former synagogue now operated by Richard Harding who later ran the most successful Chicago music cabarets. He featured avante-garde films upstairs, and many headliners, as well as new talent like Arlo Guthrie and Fred Holstein. We spent most of our time arguing politics and planning tactics. Al Raby was a good pool player. As was often the case in the civil rights movement, there were a number of love affairs. It seemed that everyone in the complex knew everybody else, a sense of community that I have not experienced since.

TAC members including Marthe picketed the management office every day, demanding negotiations. Among the marchers were usually mothers with their baby carriages, carrying signs. Marthe's pregnancy became more apparent as the summer months went by.

At one weekly meeting of the Chicago Federation of Tenants Unions, someone from JOIN ("Jobs or Income Now"), a community organization in Uptown, proposed that only tenants should represent their organizations at future meetings. We looked around the room. There were organizers from four public-housing projects and an East Garfield Park union, and a big delegation from JOIN. There were a few SCLC staff members, volunteer law students and union organizers, and McCullough and myself from TAC. We were the only tenants there.

Rennie Davis, a leader from the Students for a Democratic Society working with JOIN, argued forcefully for the idea that only tenants from tenants' organizations should attend these meetings, bespectacled and earnest. Bernardine Dohrn, a University of Chicago law student, gave principled support. She was seated high up and wearing a miniskirt. I spoke against the motion: As a practical matter, this federation was working well, and while more effort should be made to have tenant representatives come to meetings, we should simply work toward that goal.

I lost the vote overwhelmingly. Even McCullough voted for it. The next week when we went to the meeting we were the only ones there. They had in effect voted themselves out of the federation. But McCullough continued to work closely with the SCLC staff and the other unions, especially in East Garfield Park, where activists were organizing the tenants of particular slum landlords.

Reverend James Bevel, Dr. King's point man for the Chicago campaign, had set as his primary goal to organize in the ghetto – to empower the powerless – but for the first six months it appeared that Mayor Richard J. Daley was winning the battle of public opinion. These outsiders were complaining about slums? He announced new measures to deal with dilapidated housing, first a plan to tear down thousands of slum buildings, then a plan to increase inspection so housing would have to be brought up to code, and finally a bond issue for general improvements on the West Side. Quite a departure from a year earlier, when he famously declared, "There are no slums in Chicago."

Daley also had the loyalty of the black Democratic machine on the city's South Side. The "Black Belt" had elected the first black congressman after Reconstruction, and that proud First Congressional District was now represented by William Dawson, a powerful member of the machine. So Bevel found it much more feasible to organize on the West Side, where the only black alderman, Ben Lewis, had been shot and killed gangland style three years before. He was found on the carpet of his office, hands cuffed behind his back and shot twice in the back of the head. Witnesses said the same policemen who carried out the execution investigated the case.

Bevel arranged for Dr. King to move into an apartment in East Garfield Park, where his security was handled by the Chicago chapter of the Deacons for Defense and Justice.

The SCLC's efforts led to the formation of scores of new organizations, including six well-organized tenants unions. But all in all, by July the movement had stalled. So Dr. King announced a new phase of the campaign, to be launched with a rally at Soldier Field on July 10th and a march to City Hall. He had decided on a new strategy.

The over-all movement was to be a merger of Dr. King's Southern Christian Leadership Conference and Raby's Coordinating Council of Community Organizations, but from the very beginning, at planning meetings in the fall of 1965, there was a cultural clash. Chicago's civil rights movement had been focused on the "de facto" segregation of the city's schools and the discriminatory policies of the school superintendent, Ben Willis, who piled up what came to be called "Willis Wagons" on the playgrounds of black schools rather than assign students to nearby white schools. School integration was their main goal. But Willis was resigning in August, and school integration did not appeal to SCLC leaders like Jim Bevel. They were talking about dispersing the black community. He was interested in empowering it.

That tension is well described in *"Confronting the Color Line"* by Alan Anderson and George Pickering, a study of the Chicago campaign. So Dr. King chose a third way. Not school integration, not black empowerment, but desegregation. "The desegregationist principle provided a middle way," they wrote. "The black minority was to be mobilized, to be sure, but around the general theme of an open city, beginning with the desegregation of the real estate market." He had settled on the basic strategy too: marches to real estate offices that were practicing discrimination.

The American Friends Service Committee had done extensive research on Chicago's segregated housing, beginning with the 1951 race riots in Cicero. They had documented the fact that the dual housing market victimized blacks with higher rents and worse conditions. Bernard Lafayette led the effort that spring to gather evidence against specific realtors who discriminated, sending first white then black teams to try to buy homes. Marches to those agents' offices for prayer vigils could show to the world how the walls of the ghetto were enforced.

The July 10th Soldier Field rally drew some 40,000 people on a sweltering Sunday afternoon as Dr. King announced his campaign to create an "open city." Al Raby spoke, as did Floyd McKissick, national director of the Congress on Racial Equality, expressing his organization's solidarity, and James Meredith, fresh from his Mississippi march.[2] Dr. King said the campaign was going into the

---

[2] Meredith, the first black to attend the University of Mississippi, led a voter-registration march in June of 1966 with a few of his friends from Memphis, Tennessee to Jackson, Mississippi. He was wounded by a shotgun blast June 9th, and the following day Dr. King, McKissick of CORE, and Stokely Carmichael, head of the Student Nonviolent Coordinating Committee (SNCC), announced they would all join in the march, which by its end had grown to nearly 15,000. At a June 26th victory rally, at the end of a successful voter-registration drive, Carmichael delivered his call for "black power."

mobilization phase. We would strive to create on open city of brotherly love. He also said the day would come when Chicago would elect a black mayor, a prophesy fulfilled 17 years later when Harold Washington was elected.

After the rally Dr. King led a march of thousands from Soldier Field to City Hall and posted the Chicago Freedom Movement's demands on the locked door, just as his namesake Martin Luther had posted his call for church reforms on the cathedral door centuries before. There was a detailed list including calls for an end to discrimination in employment, the recognition of welfare unions, the desegregation of teachers, the publication of achievement scores and the creation of a citizens review board for grievances against police brutality. But first and foremost, the goal was for an open city.

"For our primary target we have chosen housing. As of July 10 we shall cease to be accomplices to a housing system of discrimination, segregation and degradation. We shall begin to act as if Chicago were an open city. We shall act on the basis that every man is entitled to full access of buying or renting housing that is sound, attractive and reasonably priced."[3] There followed steps to be taken by the real estate industry and governmental agencies, including a call for the 1966 Civil Rights Act to include a strong federal ban on all housing discrimination.

Dr. King was ready to start the marches that weekend, but plans were interrupted when a riot broke out on the West Side. That Tuesday afternoon was another

---

[3] *Chicago Sun-Times*, July 11, 1966.

scorching day, and a group of black kids were playing in the fire hydrant spray on the Near West Side when police moved in and closed off the hydrant. They could see Italian kids playing at their open hydrants just a few blocks away, so they, joined by neighbors, turned the hydrant back on. When the police returned they were pelted with bottles and rocks. From that small incident things escalated over the coming nights into full-scale rioting across the West Side, with arson, looting, two black people dead and the National Guard patrolling the streets. Dr. King tried frantically to keep the peace, but was sometimes met with indifference.

Basil Talbott and I wrote a story for Sunday's paper describing the growing black community on the West Side that now extended to the city limits, and recounting the event that set off the riot the previous summer, when a firetruck hit and killed a demonstrator who was protesting at an all-white fire station. But we, and Hugh Hough who wrote the main story, didn't know about a meeting Dr. King had had at the height of the riot.

In his book *"At Canaan's Edge"* Taylor Branch gives Andrew Young's account of a long meeting between Dr. King and two West Side gang leaders as representatives of the U.S. Justice Department waited patiently for their turn. The gang leaders would tell stories of injustices inflicted upon their community by the police, and Dr. King would describe the brutality of southern policemen to civil rights demonstrators, bringing Ralph Abernathy into the discussion of bad times. They also shared stories about black preachers who preyed on their parishioners. Young relates how Dr. King continued to preach nonviolence, and how at the end of their meeting the leader of the Roman Saints gave a speech describing the tactics and philosophy of nonviolence, and he went on to engineer a pact with other gang leaders to give the tactic a try.

The following week the marches to real estate offices began, and each time the line of march was attacked by angry white mobs. On August 6th, Dr. King was hit in the head with a rock while joining a prayer vigil at a real estate company in Marquette Park. The picture of the Nobel Peace Prize winner bent over in pain made worldwide news. "I have never seen such hate – not in Mississippi or Alabama – as I see here in Chicago," he said. "This is a terrible thing."[4]

TAC voted to go on a rent strike on August 1st. There were 628 apartments, so the lost revenue would be considerable. On the advice of our union and legal advisers, McCullough arranged to have the rents put in escrow. He also arranged to have the New York chapter of CORE picket the offices of Rapid America, the corporation that owned our complex. We demanded that the owners negotiate. "Back TAC" was our slogan. August 1st came and went and then, a week later, they evicted three steering committee members, stacking their furniture on the grass by the sidewalk on Hudson Street.

McCullough led a delegation to meet with the Freedom Movement leaders to enlist their support, and met some stiff resistance. Jesse Jackson argued that Old Town Gardens did not represent the slums that were the focus of the campaign and the poor black people who needed empowerment. Al Raby argued in favor of supporting us,

---

[4] *Chicago Sun-Times*, August 6, 1966: 1.

saying we represented the kind of racial integration the movement was striving for. McCullough argued that the owners had decided to turn the complex into a slum, and that this case illustrated the whole dual housing market problem. The discussion lasted for many hours, with McCullough pointing out that the East Garfield Park tenants union had gained a collective bargaining contract with a West Side slum landlord, and that there were three other strong tenants unions in housing projects. A victory by TAC would help the whole tenant movement.

The next night Dr. King came to our rally at the nearby Olivet Community Center, jammed with some 700 tenants and supporters. "What we have here is the anatomy of the development of a slum" he said, according to the Sun-Times. "We mean to stop it in its tracks right now." He pledged the full support of the SCLC and the CCCO, and said a victory here would help rent strikes across the city. "In order to get labor organized, labor had to make sacrifices and go to jail and make considered judgments to break injunctions," he said. "We have troops in Chicago ready to go to jail with you."[5]

After Dr. King left, McCullough announced that we were going to move the evicted tenants back into their apartments. We marched out of the center and around the corner and moved them back in, with a human chain from the sidewalk to their apartments, singing "We Shall Overcome," and especially the verse, "We shall not be moved." Security guards were blocked from interfering by

---

[5] *Chicago Sun-Times*, "Rent Strikers Sit In; Dr. King Vows Support," August, 1966.

determined tenants. It was one of the most beautiful nights of my life.

Of course the battle had just begun, and the furniture was moved out of their apartments again. Linda Johnson, a social worker and steering committee member, became the symbol of our struggle, chaining herself to a radiator so she could not be evicted and promising to live in one of the tents McCullough had arranged to be set up behind the Olivet center. Ten TAC members were arrested at a sit-in at the management office, but Marthe was not among them. The police refused to arrest a pregnant woman.

The movement's real estate marches grew in size and number, and the hostility of the crowds on the Southwest and Northwest Sides did not abate. The police department was overworked protecting these peaceful marches and vigils from rock-throwing, insultscreaming mobs. The policemen took abuse for protecting this invasion of blacks into their neighborhood. But the marchers received the rocks and racial slurs and sexual insults. White priests and nuns were denounced as "White Niggers" and Judases. The marches and vigils continued on the Northwest Side, the Southwest Side, the Southeast Side. At one point Al Raby, Jesse Jackson and Jim Bevel led three simultaneous marches with hundreds of demonstrators each. Mayor Daley was desperate to make peace.

The Chicago Conference on Religion and Race convened a "Summit Meeting" to try to bring a resolution to the crisis. On August 17, sixty-eight delegates gathered around a giant horseshoe table at the Cathedral House of St.

James Episcopal Church in downtown Chicago. There were Mayor Daley and top city officials, the heads of the city's largest corporations, real estate companies and financial institutions. There were Dr. King and Al Raby and other civil rights leaders, union heads and religious leaders. It was an unprecedented gathering of the city's power brokers.

Ben Heineman, head of the Northwestern Railroad, chaired the all-day session, selected because he had chaired the White House Conference on Civil Rights in June. The movement presented its list of 14 demands to bring about open housing. Mayor Daley immediately agreed to all the demands on the city, including enforcement of a 1963 open housing ordinance. Others followed suit in pledging support, except for the Chicago Real Estate Board, which argued that agents were simply carrying out the wishes of clients. Dr. King and Al Raby challenged them to show leadership.

During the luncheon recess, Mayor Daley told Ross Beatty, president of the Real Estate Board that he had to make concessions "in the interests of the city of Chicago." That afternoon Beatty announced that the Real Estate Board would support open housing legislation at the state level, provided that the laws were binding on homeowners as well as real estate agents.

The negotiations dragged on into the night, with everyone agreeing in principle with open housing, and the civil rights leaders trying to pin down governmental agencies and the real estate and mortgage industries with specific, measurable steps. Finally Heineman brought the session to a close by saying he would appoint a subcommittee to report back to the group nine days later. The Sun-Times headline called it a "Sincere, Fruitful" meeting, but noted the marches would continue.

Continue they did, even after Daley obtained an injunction to limit them to one march a day of no more than 500 people. Dr. King announced that the next Sunday, two days after the Summit was set to meet again, he would lead a march of 2,000 into Cicero, long known as a bastion of white racism. Daley's injunction did not cover the suburbs.

On Thursday, August 26, Dr. King and the Chicago Freedom Movement accepted the Summit Agreement with Mayor Daley and the city's civic elite, and agreed to stop the demonstrations. The Sun-Times headline proclaimed "Historic Pact: Freedom of Residence." The photos above showed a happy Mayor Daley, a proud Ben Heineman and a thoughtful looking Dr. King. The delegates, after much debate, had accepted the subcommittee's report, which was an elaboration of the original movement demands. It detailed steps to be taken by government and commerce to establish fair housing. Copies of the city's fair housing ordinance would be posted in every real estate office. A permanent agency would be formed to coordinate the desegregation efforts.

Of course enforcement would depend on the good faith of all the parties. But that document and the enforcement efforts of the permanent agency, called the Leadership Council for Metropolitan Open Communities, provided an important blueprint for how housing desegregation could be carried out.

Both Dr. King and Mayor Daley were immediately attacked for selling out. Two angry civil rights leaders announced they would march on Cicero anyway. Mayor Daley's City Hall was picketed the next day by furious whites. But Mayor Daley was delighted that he had finally ended the marches.

Marthe and I joined a group from TAC to support Dr. King as he presented the Summit Agreement at a meeting at Liberty Baptist Church. Halfway through his talk a group of hecklers started shouting at him from the back of the church, so he invited one of them to come up and speak. Monroe Sharp from the Student Non-violent Coordinating Committee, a major player in the civil rights movement, gave a convincing argument that the agreement was not going to improve the daily lives of black people. Not marching to Cicero showed the movement had been tricked again, he said, and the black community didn't have to beg Mayor Daley for anything.

Dr. King rose to respond, but rather than deal with any specific issue, he spoke about justice, quoting one of his favorite passages from a poem: "Truth forever on the scaffold, Wrong forever on the throne, Yet that scaffold sways the future…." His passion won a thunderous ovation from the joyous, smiling crowd.[6]

The march on Cicero did take place a week later, led by Chester Robinson of the West Side Organization and Bob Lucas of the Kenwood-Oakland Community

---

[6] King would often quote this poem "This Present Crisis," written by James Russell Lowell in 1844.

Conference. Police and the National Guard protected some 250 marchers against a white mob of thousands. "6 Bayoneted, 42 arrested" was the headline. It was an embarrassment for Dr. King.

A week later, after an all-night bargaining session, I was returning home at 4 a.m. when waiting for me in my building entranceway was Basil Talbot, my reporter friend. The building owners and the TAC negotiators had agreed that no one would talk about the settlement until our press conference later that day, but Talbot managed to weasel it out of me, arguing that the last edition had gone to press. So I told him that we had won! Rapid America had agreed to sell to the Community Renewal Society, a church-supported non-profit. Talbot proceeded to run to a phone, and the last edition of the Sun-Times that morning had the story on page three. It was, Talbot wrote, "another victory for Dr. Martin Luther King and the Southern Christian Leadership Conference."[7]

That's really the end of the story. Dr. King went on to try to forge an alliance between the civil rights and anti-Vietnam War movements. In one of the most important speeches of his life, April 4, 1967 at the Riverside Church in New York, Dr. King argued that the two causes were necessarily linked. Stokely Carmichael, who had been urging him to take this position for the past year, was seated in the front row as Dr. King spoke.

"A time comes when silence is betrayal," he said. Young rioters had countered his pleas for nonviolence by

____

[7] *Chicago Sun-Times,* September 9, 1966: 3.

saying our country itself relied on massive doses of violence. "Their questions hit home, and I realized that I could never again raise my voice against the violence of the oppressed in the ghettos without having first spoken clearly to the greatest purveyor of violence in the world today -- my own government."

"We are called upon to speak for the weak, for the voiceless, for the victims of our nation, for those it calls enemies," he said. "No document from human hands can make these humans any less our brothers."

He called for an immediate halt to the bombing in Vietnam and a unilateral cease fire. Many were angered by the speech, especially in the White House, but also among many civil rights leaders, who feared it would weaken the movement. But it had a major impact in mobilizing the anti-war movement. O n April 15th, Dr. King led an anti-war march in New York of hundreds of thousands, the largest demonstration to date. Dr. King was planning a Poor People's March on Washington and supporting striking garbage workers in Memphis when he was assassinated on April 4, 1968, exactly one year after the Riverside speech.

TAC lived on for a year and a half, carrying our precinct for Dick Gregory, comedian and political activist, when he ran for mayor against Daley. We beat back a challenge from a black power group in two elections and changed owners when the Community Renewal Society refused our demand for a cooperative. They wanted to use section 221 D3 of the housing act, intended to provide housing for moderate-income people. Our surveys showed that more than half of our tenants didn't qualify.[8]

The Maremont Foundation agreed to help us, but lost control of the complex over the Christmas holiday of 1967, when the Arthur Rubloff company foreclosed on its second mortgage. Apparently the Maremont lawyers had missed a deadline. Rubloff turned the complex to 221 D3 housing.

In the summer of 1968 Marthe and I and our one-year-old son moved to South Shore, one of the city's few integrated communities. Marthe went to work for the Leadership Council.

Dr. King's Chicago campaign was widely seen as a failure. According to Branch's biography, Dr. King's longtime friend and associate at the SCLC Ralph Abernathy said "We should have known better." And Bayard Rustin said "I knew he had to fall on his face." The book *Confronting the Color Line* is subtitled "The broken promise of the civil rights movement in Chicago."

But I think history will judge the Chicago campaign differently.

Dr. King mobilized a broader civil rights movement in Chicago, including labor unions, neighborhood organizations, churches and new civic organizations. That movement defeated State's Attorney Edward Hanrahan in 1972 because of his role in the assassination of Black Panther

---

[8] We just couldn't understand why a church-backed organization would oppose our efforts to become a cooperative. But in the opinion of their real estate expert, assistance should be aimed only at the poorest black communities.

leader Fred Hampton. Eleven years later that coalition was key to the election of Harold Washington as Chicago's first black mayor.

But most importantly, Dr. King's Chicago campaign led to passage of the national Fair Housing Act of 1968. It took Dr. King's assassination, and the riots the next day in 100 American cities, to finally accomplish his Chicago goal.

As Branch puts it, "A remorseful Congress passed the nondiscrimination bill for housing transactions one day after what amounted to a state funeral in Atlanta, with the casket wagon drawn by mules." Still, Branch fails to make the connection to the Chicago campaign.

That bill has had an important impact on housing nationwide, making it possible for many more black families to buy decent housing. That they mostly chose to live in black communities was a great disappointment to many progressive whites. But Dr. King was not an integrationist, but a desegregationist.

This distinction was made clear during the Summit negotiations with Mayor Daley when one of the spokesmen for Dr. King's side was trying to pin the Real Estate Board down on a goal of having black families on every block. One of King's aides abruptly changed the subject and spoke of empowerment. The idea of this kind of a black dispersal was the last thing Dr. King had in mind. In fact, it seems to imply the hope that blacks would dissolve into the white community.[9]

If he had come to Chicago to support the CCCO, the goal would have been to integrate the schools. But in the list posted on the door at City Hall in July, the only education demands were to desegregate teachers and publish test scores.

Dr. King chose Bevel to lead his campaign because he was dedicated to empowering the black community. Dr. King's goal in Chicago became to break down the walls of the ghetto by opening up housing.

The civil rights movement had accomplished the desegregation of public accommodations and established voting rights in the South. Now, with Dr. King's death, it had won fair housing.

---

[9] The source is John McKnight, who was at the time the Midwest director of the U.S. Civil Rights Commission and an observer at the meetings. The interpretation is my own.

Chapter 2

Martin, Bobby and Fred

The King Riots

When Dr. King was assassinated on April 4th, 1968 my wife and I were still living at Old Town Gardens, and my parents and their extended family, including my sisters Mardi and Connie, Connie's husband David Ward and their baby Sarah were all living on Fifth Avenue in the middle of the West Side ghetto. They were part of a project by the nearby Ecumenical Institute to plant "stakes" in the neighborhood to help bring about revitalization.

The next afternoon riots broke out nearby on Madison Street. High school students, incensed by the lack of tributes to Dr. King at their schools, marched from school to school in their own tribute, gathering more students as they headed west, until they numbered in the thousands when they marched toward Austin High School, on the far West Side. It was a peaceful march, in the spirit of Dr. King, with parade marshals, and many wearing the front page picture of the slain leader from the Sun-Times that morning.

There were black students at the integrated Austin, but it was in a white neighborhood, and the sight of so many young blacks, mostly boys, caused alarm. Three squad cars arrived to block the line of march, and a police lieutenant fired his pistol in the air to disperse the crowd.

That was the spark that ignited the West Side riot. What an irony that Dr. King had led marches into white neighborhoods, and now this tribute was met with police with guns. The students retreated to Madison Street, and some started breaking windows and looting white-owned stores. The fury mounted, and some stores were set on fire, then every nearby white-owned store.

My father called me that afternoon at the Sun-Times and we discussed what to do. It seemed safest for the family to stay in the house. David had driven out to Oak Park to take Mardi home from her job as a social worker, and his car had been rocked on the ramp to the expressway by angry young blacks, but they were now safely home.

But later that night, as they watched neighbors returning home with TV sets and stereos, they could see flames in the distance. Then the house behind them caught on fire, and my parents decided to move to the Ecumenical Institute building. They were given friendly greetings from neighbors when all six walked over to the institute, Connie bringing bottles and diapers for the baby in a pillow case.

The staff members were in a meeting, and as the family waited in the basement while a class was going on, a group of six black men rushed down the stairs, and the leader, waving a revolver, announced that they were going to burn down the whole building, a white outpost in their community. Then another invader recognized my father, and came over to talk to him. My father calmly introduced Doug

Andrews, head of the Garfield Organization, to each family member. Andrews led them out the door to safety.

The subway was closed, but they were able to flag down a cab on the Eisenhower Expressway nearby, and they spent the night at a downtown YMCA. The experience terrorized family members, and led my father to reconsider the role of white people in the black community. Doug Andrews helped the family move to an apartment in Hyde Park, and then was arrested. A fringe member of the group had been a police infiltrator.

Meanwhile my wife had watched the looting of the cleaner's across the street from our apartment, and we and our baby son spent the night in a spare bedroom of City Editor Jim Hoge. I wrote a long story about the riot for the next Sunday paper, describing in detail how it started.[10]

Reporter Ben Heineman, Jr. followed on Monday with an explosive story showing that at least four of the nine black men killed that night were deliberately shot down by police.[11] Mayor Daley responded with his famous "shoot to kill" order for arsonists, and "shoot to maim" order for looters, apparently in an effort to prevent any investigation.[12]

---

[10] Christopher Chandler, *Chicago Sun-Times*. April 14, 1968.

[11] His findings were incorporated into a general story by rewrite man Jon Anderson, but he was able to tell the full story the next February in the Chicago Journalism Review ("Why silence shrouds the four who died," Vol.2, No. 2: 3).

[12] Christopher Chandler, "'Shoot to Kill...Shoot to Maim.'" *Chicago Reader* April 4, 2002. Web. January 4, 2017.

My father was among a group of clergymen who met with Daley to ask that he rescind those orders. My father told him it was a matter of moral necessity. Daley did rescind the orders the following day, saying he meant when an act of dangerous arson could not be stopped any other way, and claiming that he had only said "shoot to detain" looters.

Daley never forgave dad for preaching to him. He referred to my father afterward as "that rioter" and succeeded in forcing him out of town within a few months. My father certainly wasn't a rioter, but he was a dangerous man. He had brought the Ecumenical Institute to Chicago from Texas, and the Garfield Organization was a neighborhood group partially funded, as were many others, by the Church Federation. He was among those who invited Dr. King to Chicago in 1966.[13]

The Kennedy Campaign.

Bobby Kennedy had announced he was running for president, and was campaigning in Indiana in his first primary the day that Dr. Martin Luther King was assassinated. He was scheduled to speak in the black community in Indianapolis that evening, and many warned

---

[13] Dr. Edgar H.S. Chandler was executive director of the Church Federation of Greater Chicago from 1960 to 1968, after serving for ten years as head of refugee resettlement for the World Council of Churches (see Wikipedia). It wasn't until a year before he died in 1998 that he told me how Mayor Daley had pressed him to leave Chicago. Daley talked to some of the city's leading businessmen, who were also the primary supporters of the Church Federation. The business leaders met at the Commercial Club over lunch and decided to earmark their support for programs and to stop all funding of neighborhood or civic organizations. When they presented their plan, dad resigned and took a position as head of the Worcester, Massachusetts Council of Churches.

him not to go. But he went and announced Dr. King's death to the crowd. He gave a truly inspired speech, comparing King's death to that of his brother John, and quoting Aeschylus:

"Even in our sleep, pain which cannot forget falls drop by drop upon the heart, until, in our own despair, against our will, comes wisdom through the awful grace of God."

He told the crowd that all of us, black and white, must follow Dr. King's quest for brotherly love and understanding, and once more cited the ancient Greeks who sought to "tame the savageness of man and make gentle the life of the world." Indianapolis was the only American city that did not have a riot the following night.

I was asked by Professor Richard Wade of the University of Chicago to head up press relations for the Kennedy campaign for Northwest Indiana. I took a leave of absence from the Sun-Times and commuted each day to the campaign office in downtown Gary. The primary was scheduled for May 7th, and Kennedy was trailing his two competitors, Sen. Eugene McCarthy and the Indiana governor Roger D. Branigin, the stand-in for President Johnson.

McCarthy had the support of most liberals for his brave challenge to President Johnson in the New Hampshire primary, where his anti-Vietnam War stance earned him a close second. Branigin had the support of the democratic organization and was a popular governor.

My wife and I had become disillusioned with McCarthy after attending a rally at the Blackstone Hotel. An overflow crowd, many activists against the Vietnam War, listened to a long speech that barely mentioned Vietnam, or foreign affairs of any kind. He also didn't mention civil rights. We turned to Bobby Kennedy, who was promising to end the war on his first day as president. After the Dr. King speech, we were fully committed.

The Kennedy strategy in Indiana was to stand for the end of the war and the furthering of civil rights, and to take strong populist stands on issues like poverty, labor rights and improvements to the environment. He challenged steel company executives, to their faces, to take responsibility for the pollution they created. He challenged college students who supported the Vietnam War to admit they were privileged by their draft deferments, and said it was the poorest people carrying the burden of that war.

In Gary, my assignment was to go after the white ethnic vote of the surrounding communities. Kennedy already had strong support in the black community and from Gary Mayor Richard Hatcher, the first black mayor of a Northern city. But the region was racially polarized, and many whites had been frightened by the nationwide King riots.

My first act was to make thousands of copies of a column by Tom Fitzpatrick of the Sun-Times that described a poignant moment of Bobby's campaign. They were included in all our campaign packets. Then we advertised and provided stories and pictures to all the different ethnic newspapers. Bobby paraded with Tony Zale, the former boxing champ from nearby, and brought in his sister-in-law, Princess Radziwill, for a motorcade. She was Jackie Kennedy's sister, and had married a Polish prince. Ted Kennedy came by to hold a press conference.

I arranged for Bobby to be interviewed by the host of the most popular radio show in the area, with country and western music and red neck commentary. The host was overwhelmed that Kennedy himself had come to his little studio in Merrillville, and the half-hour interview was a very friendly discussion, with Kennedy stressing that he had been the chief U.S. law enforcement official as Attorney General. He talked about how the steel companies were polluting the area and took a strong stand in favor of union rights. The host was so proud of the interview he replayed it the day before the primary. A small factor, but we won that primary going away.

I admired the whole Kennedy operation, with its brain trust in Indianapolis that included Pierre Salinger, and its ground operation that included advance men like Bill Haddad who prepared every detail of an upcoming event. I admired Kennedy, an introverted, deeply religious man who could speak forcefully of building a brighter future.

When I shook his hand it was calloused from the thousands of handshakes of the campaign. I had led him through a deserted kitchen at that small radio station, a memory that came back when he was shot and killed in a kitchen the night he won the California primary a month later. The two men I admired most had been assassinated in two months.

I believe Bobby Kennedy would have made a truly great president. More than ending the war in Vietnam, he would have changed the country's whole stance in the world. He had learned while working for his brother John that peace was possible, as described in Jim Douglass's important book, *"J.F.K. And the Unspeakable."* That book documents John Kennedy's decisions to withdraw from Vietnam, curb the power of the CIA and end the Cold War, decisions that angered what President Eisenhower had called "the military-industrial complex."

Bobby Kennedy was also dedicated to "healing the racial wounds" with new programs that would bring about true equality. It's interesting to note that, according to National Opinion Research Center studies, a healthy majority of white Americans supported ending the Vietnam War and strengthening civil rights at that time.

Bobby was shot and killed the night he won the California primary and was assured of the Democratic nomination. Judging by public opinion polls, he would have been easily elected president.

Fred Hampton

On the morning of Dec. 4, 1969, John Kiffner of the New York Times and I were among the many who toured the West Side apartment where Fred Hampton had been killed in a raid that early morning.

Our guide, a young disciplined member of the Black Panthers, first showed us the wave of machine gun bullets into the living room wall. Then he pointed out the shotgun blasts fired in from two different directions, and then the bedroom and the bloody mattress where Hampton had been shot while sleeping next to his pregnant wife. Howard Saffold of the Afro American Patrolman's League called it an assassination. Bobby Rush, Hampton's fellow leader in the party, went into hiding.

Kiffner wrote about the case for the Times. We at the Chicago Journalism Review put out a special issue devoted to the killing, with a full-page cover by Pulitzer Prize-winning cartoonist Bill Mauldin showing bullets fired through a door in the form of a Swastika.[14] We helped pressure the Sun-Times to finally send another reporter to the scene and expose the false evidence that State's Attorney Edward Hanrahan had paraded in a front-page article in the Tribune. I wrote an article for the New Republic they titled "The Black Panther Killings," in which I argued that Hampton was killed because he had become so powerful, and that the killing led all the way to the U.S. Justice Department.[15]

I only knew Hampton as a reporter, first seeing him in the spring of 1969 when my friend from the tenant union days, Dennis Cunningham, saw me returning from some assignment and brought me into a rally where Hampton was

---

[14] *Chicago Journalism Review*, "The death of Fred Hampton: A special report," December, 1969 Vol. 2, No. 12.
[15] Chris Chandler, "The Black Panther Killings." *New Republic,* Jan. 10, 1970: 21-24.

addressing a large crowd of white peace activists who had just concluded a march through the Loop. He told them they had marched for a just cause and America had to end the war. But he said there were grave problems right here in the city that had to be addressed. You could walk from there to areas of desperate poverty. Should that not be a priority? The audience was totally silent, chastised.

I was very impressed. I later learned Hampton had formed the first "Rainbow Coalition" of black, white and Latino street gangs and the Students for a Democratic Society. [16] He had set up a free breakfast for children program, which was feeding thousands of hungry young students on their way to school, and a free health clinic.

He was invited to the lavish Oak Brook home of Michael Butler, the producer of the musical *"Hair,"* and ended up in a long debate with Tommy Smothers of Smothers Brothers fame. Photographer Paul Sequeira made a tape of that conversation, and Hampton wins the debate again and again. He is bold, self-depreciating and open to any new good ideas.

I wrote a story that fall quoting Hampton as condemning the Weatherman's upcoming "Days of Rage." He said their announced plans to rampage in downtown Chicago were "Custeristic." I agreed with him that the plans were highly dangerous, playing into the hands of our enemies, and was happy to be able to quote him in the Sun-

---

[16] The Students for a Democratic Society was one of the most important forces in the 1960's, along with the Student Non-violent Coordinating Committee.

Times. [17] Just weeks after those demonstrations he was killed.

It was Hanrahan's State's Attorney's police who had carried out the raid that killed Black Panthers Fred Hampton and Mark Clark in an early morning raid Dec. 4th, 1969. Hanrahan's claim there had been a gun battle was disproved by evidence at the scene, and when he tried to prove shots were fired by Panthers in a front page exclusive in the Tribune, the Sun-Times countered by showing that what he was claiming as bullet holes were actually nail holes. Ballistics experts later established that police fired over 90 shots, and the Panthers one. [18]

Hampton was only 21, ten years younger than me, but I very much respected and admired him. The clear fact that our government had killed him made me and many others much more suspicious of President Nixon, and of the prior assassinations.

***

Earlier that year, State Representative Harold Washington had introduced legislation to establish a

---

[17] *Chicago Sun-Times*, "The Panthers Stay Aloof," October 9, 1969: 4.

[18] Deborah Johnson married Fred in a Panther ceremony, and was eight months pregnant. She was sleeping next to him when he was shot. They shot him again to make sure. I invited her to speak at my journalism class at Northwestern University College after assigning students to read about the case. She told them that they had been betrayed by their head of security, who drugged Fred the night before and gave the FBI a map showing where he slept. He received a bonus after the shooting. One of the students asked her what she admired most about Fred. "His arrogance," she replied. Hampton was not afraid of anything.

Citizen's Review Board for the Chicago Police Department, working with Renault Robinson, executive director of the Afro-American Patrolmen's League. Robinson had become a folk hero in the black community for his efforts to stop police brutality and increase minority hiring, and for staying on the force despite obvious punishment. Now he was working with Washington to set up a citizen board that could investigate police misconduct.

Mayor Daley was furious. The legislation went nowhere, and, according to Dempsey Travis' authorized biography, *"Harold; the People's Mayor,"* Daley told Washington's committeeman, Congressman Ralph Metcalfe, that Washington had to be dumped. Washington was one of Metcalfe's best precinct captains and organizers. He told Daley he would have to do it himself.

Metcalfe relayed the conversation to Washington, who immediately called Jack Touhy, Speaker of the Illinois House. Touhy knew what an able legislator Washington was. He told Washington he would take care of it, Travis relates, and Washington was able to survive. But Daley never forgave him.

The 70's

In 1971 I was asked by my friend Stanley Hallett to join Richard Friedman's campaign to unseat Mayor Richard J. Daley. Hallett was a minister with a doctorate in urban planning and one of the most creative people I've ever met. Friedman was running as a Republican but he was a liberal lawyer who pledged to end the corruption of the Daley machine. We used to joke, "Is Chicago ready for a single Jewish parachutist," but Friedman was able to gather some surprising independent support, especially from those angered by Daley's "shoot to kill" order and the police brutality at the 1968 Democratic Convention.

I was put in charge of "advance," and my most elaborate project for the candidate was for him to spend three days walking down Western Avenue, the longest street in the country, spending the nights with a German family, a black family and a Polish family. The welcoming black family was that of Doug Andrews, the head of the Garfield Organization and the man who had led my family to safety during the King riots.

He and the five other raiders of the Ecumenical Institute that night had all been arrested shortly after the riot. Their volunteer driver turned out to be an undercover policeman, and photos of the group setting fire to selected white targets, taken by a photographer proud to chronicle the uprising, were in the hands of police.

But in their remarkable trial in 1969, all five were found innocent of all counts by an all-white jury. Eugene Pinchem, who later became a distinguished Appellate Court judge, led a team of five lawyers who managed to demolish the state's case.

My father was a character witness for Andrews, but the key emotional factor was that the main prosecution witness, the undercover policeman, had done nothing to aid a white women who was being pummeled by an angry mob, while Edward "Fats" Crawford, the leader of the arsonists, had waded into the crowd and carried her to safety.

The jury knew they had probably set a few fires among the hundreds that night, but they hadn't hurt anybody. Witnesses that were supposed to be victims praised them, and they certainly weren't the conspirators who caused the whole riot, as the prosecution was claiming. After the innocent verdicts were read, the jury, the defendants and the defense lawyers all went to celebrate together at a nearby restaurant. One of these defense lawyers was James Montgomery, who would later become the city's Corporation Counsel.

Andrews was grateful that my father had testified at the trial and so was happy to cooperate with the campaign. Friedman spent the second night in his home. "Fats" Crawford, who headed the Chicago chapter of Deacons for Defense and Justice, provided security. In fact the more I learned about Crawford the more I respected him. He had formed a legally-armed group to protect black leaders after the gangland execution of his alderman, Ben Lewis, in 1963.[19] He had provided security for Dr. King during his 1966 Chicago campaign. What a paradox that he was the one who had also led the raid that terrorized my family.

The Friedman walk was getting excellent news coverage until the third night when he addressed a large Southwest Side crowd. They wanted to know if he supported

---

[19] Crawford headed the Chicago branch of the Deacons for Defense and Justice, which originated when Southern church leaders took up arms to protect their property from white supremacists who were burning down black churches.

scattered-site public housing, then being launched by the Chicago Housing Authority as a result of the Gautreaux decision in a civil rights case that had found CHA guilty of deliberate segregation.

I had urged him to express reservations. The program had little support in the black community, and other measures to compensate for past discriminatory practices should be explored. But the rest of the staff, including Hallett, felt the scattered- site policy had to be supported as a civil rights issue.

So Friedman, ever the lawyer, tried to equivocate. The crowd got increasingly angry, finally shouting in unison "Yes or No? Yes or No?" He still wouldn't commit himself, so they booed him off the stage. The campaign collapsed that night. He received 30 per cent of the vote.

On May 11, 1971, State Rep. Harold Washington led a walkout of black legislators when Vice President Spiro Agnew addressed the Illinois General Assembly. Agnew had been going around the country attacking liberals in general and the liberal press in particular. He called them "nattering nabobs of negativism." He was becoming a hero to the far right.

As he was about to address the assembly, Washington led ten black legislators on the walkout, telling the press outside Agnew was "anti-Black, anti-student, anti-peace. He's like the Ku Klux Klan, he's anti everything."

In the 1972 democrat convention, forces led by Jesse Jackson and alderman Bill Singer managed to replace the

Daley delegation, resulting in a deep divide within the local Democratic Party.

The Black Community Rebels

When Edward V. Hanrahan ran for reelection as Cook County State's Attorney in 1972, activists in the black community did not forget his role in the '69 raid that claimed the lives of Panthers Fred Hampton and Mark Clark. For the first time in memory the black community rebelled against the Democratic machine and voted overwhelmingly for his opponent, bringing an upset victory to Republican Bernard Carey.

Chicago Daily News columnist Lu Palmer wrote that the election was the "awakening" of the black community, which made his editors so nervous the column was pulled for the next edition. After another battle with his editor, he called a press conference to announce he was quitting and would never again work for a white editor.

Gary Rivlin, in his *"Fire on the Prairie,"* describes what happened next. "Anticipating trouble, he called on a few friends to help him remove his files from the building. A half dozen Black Panthers, dressed in full regalia – black berets, dark sunglasses, black leather gloves – helped Palmer carry his belongings out of the News."[20] Palmer went on to run his own magazine, and then become the most popular voice on black radio.

---

[20] Rivlin, "Fire on the Prairie,"

In 1973 Washington was able to gain passage of his bill to make Dr. King's birthday a state holiday. Illinois was the first state to do so. He had introduced the bill shortly after Dr. King's assassination in 1968 and worked over the years to slowly gain support. It was first observed as a national holiday in 1986.

Passage of that bill was especially important to Washington because back in 1966, when he was a recently elected state representative, he was compelled by the party to go to a meeting opposing Dr. King's Chicago campaign. Dempsey Travis describes how he made a brief, perfunctory appearance, seething with anger.

From 1976 to 1980 I was a writer and producer at Channel 2 News, and very much enjoyed working with anchorman Bill Kurtis on what we called "Focus Reports," an in-depth look at one of the major stories of the day.

In December, 1976 Mayor Richard J. Daley died unexpectedly of a heart attack. Wilson Frost was president pro tem of the council and should have been named acting mayor, but the white aldermen conspired and managed to elevate alderman Michael Bilandic instead. The black community was incensed, all the more so when Frost did not fight back.

The Committee to Elect a Black Mayor pressured Washington to run against Bilandic, but he instead supported Congressman Ralph Metcalfe. Then Metcalfe backed out, fearing the wrath of Daley, and supported lakefront liberal William Singer instead. Singer lost badly.

Washington ran against Bilandic in the April 1977 Democratic primary. His campaign was severely damaged when Don Rose, his campaign manager, quit the campaign midstream, saying Washington had refused to show him his tax returns. He ended up receiving only 11 per cent of the vote, but he took six South Side wards, and described the black vote as a "sleeping giant."

In 1979 Jane Byrne, former Consumer Services Commissioner, challenged Bilandic in the Democratic primary and won an improbable victory, thanks to Bilandic's bungling response to a record snowstorm. The black community was irate that during the storm CTA trains skipped stops in the black community to deliver whites from downtown to outlying areas. Once again black voters rose up against the machine and gave Byrne her primary victory.

Byrne ran as a reformer, pledging to get rid of the "evil cabal" that was running the city, headed by aldermen Ed Vrdolyak and Ed Burke, and Charles Swibel, director of the Chicago Housing Authority. But within months she welcomed them back.

Congressman Metcalfe died of a heart attack in 1979 and Washington was his natural successor. He was elected to Congress in 1980, eking out a victory despite the machine's all-out effort to oppose him.

He distinguished himself as a congressman, holding dramatic hearings in the South on tactics being used to suppress the black vote, and was a leader in the successful effort to extend the Voting Rights Act for ten years. He easily won reelection in 1982, winning the biggest plurality of any congressman in the country, according to biographer Dempsey Travis.

Meanwhile Jane Byrne angered the black community by replacing blacks with whites on the school board and the CHA board in a blatant appeal to white voters on the Northwest and Southwest Sides. Jesse Jackson led a boycott of her annual "ChicagoFest" at Navy Pier. Activists held a plebiscite, and Washington was the overwhelming winner to challenge Mayor Byrne.

Washington said he would run if they would register 50,000 new voters. They registered 120,000. Lu Palmer, the former newspaper reporter who had become the most respected voice on black radio, led the effort to draft Washington. His slogan was "We shall see in '83."

Chapter 3

The Primary Campaign

Off to a Slow Start

I only had one serious conversation about politics with Harold Washington. I had handled press for his announcement that he was running for mayor, and he kept me on as his press secretary. We had just finished a press conference on the far South Side supporting the steelworkers union, and it happened that his driver was late, so he took the occasion to ask me about my politics. Who was my favorite politician? he asked. "Bobby Kennedy," I replied. He was surprised. "I never understood the Kennedys," he said.

I explained that I had worked for Bobby in the Indiana presidential primary in 1968 and felt he would have made a great president. "This would be a different country if he hadn't been killed."

Washington said he had just finished a new biography of Bobby, and maybe he understood a little more about his appeal. It turned out he had read a number of books about the Kennedys, and I was embarrassed to admit I had read none of them.

I asked him which politician he respected most. He

thought for a time, and finally said, with emphasis, "Paul Robeson." I did not know much about Robeson, beyond that he was one of my mother's heroes. But since then I have come to appreciate him more, the athlete, movie star, opera singer and courageous political activist. And I have come to admire Harold more too.

He knew that I had been a reporter, familiar with how the media works. He also knew my politics and gave me free rein, within limits. I worked for him for the next two years, in the biggest political battle of my life, but he preferred to deal with me indirectly. I believe, in retrospect, that it was because I had the reporter's attitude of dealing with everyone as an equal. He was used to some deference, as a congressman and elder statesman of the black political independence movement.

Washington had delayed his announcement to the point where many activists were getting nervous. But he was waiting for State's Attorney Richard M. Daley to enter the race. He had held countless meetings on strategy with David Cantor, a Hyde Park activist, and determined that with Daley in the race he had a fighting chance. They calculated that a strong black vote, some Latino support and a sliver of whites should be enough to win the primary.

The campaign got off with a bang, with leading civil rights and community figures giving him a rousing welcome as he announced his candidacy to become the first black mayor of Chicago. Dick Simpson, a former alderman and highly respected reformer, had called and asked me to handle the press conference, and the night before some six of us stayed late in Washington's South Side congressional office for last minute preparations. Simpson had written a draft of the announcement, and Washington huddled with a young researcher named Kari Moe to make last minute changes,while campaign manager Renault Robinson and others went over the timing and the roles of other dignitaries. Late that night I wrote the press release for the morning, and dropped by City News Bureau to alert the media.

But after the press conference, and for several weeks, Zenobia Black and I sat for the most part alone in the new campaign office on the first floor of his South Side congressional office. I was the press secretary and she was to coordinate campaign volunteers. She was a school teacher who had worked in many campaigns, most recently on the ChicagoFest boycott. She would also become the wife of Timuel Black, a dean of Chicago's civil rights movement. I ate my lunches at a small soul food restaurant down the street and came to appreciate ham hocks and greens. I never saw another white man, except for occasionally a news vendor at the corner who I think was a bookie.

We never heard from Robinson, a legend in the black community for standing up to racism in the police force. He had played key roles both in the voter registration drive and in making Washington's campaign possible. For the voter registration campaign he had enlisted the help of Ed Gardner, who owned Soft Sheen, a popular hair products company. Gardner had his advertising team create very effective radio ads and paid for the time.

And it was Robinson once again who raised the first $100,000 in Washington's campaign funds, getting commitments from two black-owned banks, Seaway and Independence, according to Travis' account. But he was not a good manager. He never dealt with the campaign office.

Activists began to come by, and we would work with them as best we could. Richard Barnett, the longtime West Side political organizer and petition expert, was one of the first. Slim Coleman and several members of his "Heart of Uptown" organization came more and more frequently, and began to publish a campaign newspaper. Coleman's partner, fellow activist Helen Shiller, designed the campaign button, blue with a slight white rising sun. Zenobia recruited volunteers.

Harold asked me to invite the press to an event at the church of his friend the Rev. Al Sampson. But when the television cameras arrived there were maybe ten people in the church. The campaign was panned in the media. I remember one particularly damning story on Channel 11, where the reporter concluded that Washington couldn't even draw a crowd. Of course the crowd arrived later, and it was a fine rally by the time Harold spoke. I learned my lesson for future events. But clearly the downtown media had already discounted the campaign.

The key financial backer at that point was Ed Gardner. When Harold hired an advertising expert, Bill Zimmerman, his first act was to decide to change the campaign button. He said that orange was the best color. We did not agree, so Gardner had one of his bright young executives hold a meeting with Zimmerman, staff and activists, including Coleman and Shiller. Zimmerman said that tests had shown that orange was the most effective color, but no one else in the room agreed, and we kept the blue buttons. We all agreed on new ads Gardner had produced for black radio.

As the weeks went by our campaign events became more successful. We worked with progressive groups to support their causes, and the media had to respond. By Christmas we had established some momentum, thanks largely to strong support from the black media, especially radio and the small independent newspapers such as Nate Clay's "Metro News."

Then there was Lu Palmer, the radio host who for years was the most respected voice in the black community and had essentially created the movement that persuaded Washington to run. He and other leading black nationalists formed the Task Force for Black Political Empowerment, chaired by academic and activist Bob Starks. He was joined by Conrad Worrill, also an academic and activist, Alderman Danny Davis, a lifetime activist, and Reverend Al Sampson, a lifetime friend of Washington's. Worrill acted as liaison to campaign headquarters. The "Task Force" as we called it, carried out a whole independent operation within the black community, aimed at recruiting the poor and protecting against outside interference.

The New York Times reported that the civil case filed after the killings of Black Panthers Fred Hampton and Mark Clark had finally been settled, with the survivors of that December 4th, 1969 raid, and the families of Hampton and

Clark receiving a $1.8 million dollar settlement from the city, county and federal governments. Lawyers from the People's Law Office had discovered that the head of security for the Black Panthers had been an FBI informant, who provided the FBI with a floor plan showing where Hampton slept. They showed how the FBI had a nationwide program to destroy the Panthers. Those attorneys, Dennis Cunningham, Flint Taylor and Jeffrey Haas were joined by James Montgomery, who delivered the final argument to the jury. A full account of that long legal battle is provided in Haas's book *The Assassination of Fred Hampton.*

I asked Washington if he wanted to attend the annual observance of Hampton's death on December 4th, but he immediately declined. I agreed he might have been labeled as a radical if he had attended.

Washington was invited to appear for a taping of a New Year's Eve show at Channel 7, along with Mayor Jane Byrne and State's Attorney Richard M. Daley, the three mayoral candidates.

Daley declined the offer, but Byrne was there. At the time she was the overwhelming favorite to win reelection. She had a $10-million-dollar war chest, and had hired a top media expert from New York, David Sawyer. His cleverly crafted commercials of the "New Jane" had helped her gain a healthy lead in the polls. Washington was way behind.

The show was not to be a debate, but simply a question and answer session with the candidates about their plans for the coming year. But it turned into a heated debate, and Washington won hands down. After the half hour was over, the producer asked if we could go another half hour, since it went so well. I agreed, much to my later regret. In the second half Byrne did much better, almost holding her own. We were pleased with the event.

But when they aired the segment on New Year's Eve, they had cut it back to 30 minutes and managed to make it look like a draw, or even a Byrne edge. Harold was furious. He wanted to hold a press conference outside Channel 7 and denounce the station for blatantly distorting the encounter.

I told him we couldn't do that until we had the evidence. The press tends to stick together, and we had no proof. We would have to get a copy of both tapes and be able to show the distortion. He reluctantly agreed, but pressed me to get the evidence, fast.

The next day I was told that senior producer Dick Goldberg had edited the tape. I knew Goldberg from when we both worked at Channel 2 news, so I called him up and asked what happened. He said he didn't know what I was talking about and claimed the editing was fair. I asked if we could get a copy of the full tape, and he said he would take care of it.

He stalled, and we wrote formal requests to the station. Meanwhile, Washington didn't want to wait. He even sent intermediates to urge me to have that press conference. The station finally released the tapes a week before the primary -- way too late. They must have seen that Washington had a chance.

When the newspapers revealed that the El Rukn streetgang had been funded by the Byrne campaign, the Task Force picketed their headquarters, denouncing their betrayal of the black community.

When Richard M. Daley arrived to be endorsed by scores of black preachers on the South Side, the Task Force picketed the event. Lu Palmer and Robert Starks attended Daley's press conference and heckled him. Starks then denounced the clergymen to their faces for selling out, and the ministers, mostly church-front preachers, were cowed into submission. "We talked about the preachers like they were just dogs," Starks said.[21] It was a big story on television that day, and we at headquarters were delighted.

Raby was angry that he had not been told of the event, and worried that he would be blamed for "polarizing" the campaign that was "under his direction."

Raby was also having trouble with the finance committee, claiming that their ignorance was stopping Zimmerman from running effective commercials. Raby and Zimmerman shared the view that the two men who chaired the finance committee were "business executives who didn't know the inner workings of a political campaign."

Rivlin quotes Zimmerman as saying, "These were people who had never read a script in their lives making changes that were impossible or just plain wrong."[22] But perhaps Berry and Clark knew more than they were given

---

[21] Rivlin, "Fire on the Prairie," 138.
[22] Ibid.

credit for. The finance committee was chaired by Walter Clark, a black bank executive and longtime supporter of civil rights, and Bill Berry, longtime chairman of the Chicago Urban League and a friend of Dr. King, who he marched with in Selma.

When the candidates had their first formal debate in January, Washington beat both Byrne and Daley convincingly. It was a turning point in the campaign. For the first time a wide audience saw a candidate who was dignified, very well informed and with a progressive agenda for the city. He also had a huge vocabulary and enjoyed playing with words. He was confident and good-natured. Daley was the big loser.

Within the campaign it was consultant Tom Coffey who had made sure that Washington was well prepared for the debate. He was also the one who made sure Washington made a full disclosure about his legal troubles early on. I had told Harold that he had to do it, to avoid attacks by his opponents, but he was dragging his feet. Coffey asked me to try to persuade him.

We had a formal meeting in his congressional office, and I laid out the argument to him. He couldn't expect his opponents not to bring it up. If we made full disclosure now, we should be able to put it behind us. We might even be able to use it to our advantage considering the tax evasion charge was a clear case of political retribution, a response to the walkout he had led in the state legislature to protest the presence of Vice President Spiro Agnew. He bristled at the suggestion. "They'll be no more talk of that," he said.

But he did agree to full disclosure, and Coffey arranged for an appearance before the Rotary Club where Washington laid out the exact details of his case with elaborate charts and graphs. He had served 37 days in County Jail in 1972 for failing to file income tax returns. But he pointed out for the three years involved, the total he owed the IRS was $508. Taxes were automatically deducted from his paycheck as a state legislator, and the sum owed came only from occasional speeches. Negligent yes, but hardly criminal.

He had also had his law license suspended for a year, but again it was clearly only negligence. He reimbursed the three clients involved, none of whom had paid his full $200 down payment, but neglected to respond to authorities.

There were routine stories the following day, and the matters did not become a campaign issue in the primary.

The Turning Point

In January, Washington named civil rights leader Al Raby as his new campaign manager. The campaign moved to an old Loop office building, and new staff were hired. Kari Moe headed the issues office and gathered a staff of research volunteers. She had come to the campaign through Hal Baron, the former head of research for the Urban League, and she had an advanced degree from MIT.

A steady stream of activists visited Zenobia Black's staff, meetings were held every day in the conference room, and Raby named a blue ribbon steering committee headed by

Bill Berry, former head of the Chicago Urban League. The press office grew to some ten full-time workers, including Mark Zalkin, a full-time activist and an editor of Slim Coleman's publications, who had been preparing for a campaign against Mayor Byrne for the past year. Coleman, Zalkin and Helen Shiller were all part of a political collective, "Heart of Uptown," that was dedicated to the ideals of Fred Hampton. We used to call them "Slim and them."

As it happened, Richard M. Daley's campaign office was in the same building, and we would often share elevator rides with staffers from his campaign. One day I was on an elevator ride with Bill Daley, and we chatted briefly about the campaign. Mayor Byrne was still the overwhelming favorite, and I suggested we should both aim our fire at her. He smiled and agreed.

We held a series of issue-oriented press conferences based on Zalkin's research, backed up with research from Moe's issues office and in cooperation with progressive organizations. We held them on site, giving the TV stations their footage, and Washington made news, taking bold progressive stands.

We prepared a briefing package for Washington every morning with his daily schedule, including brief summaries of each stop, and a press release, talking points and background material on his main press event. It was an effective strategy, and we outdistanced our rivals in the major media. We had a full-time staffer getting radio feeds for the black media every day. A Puerto-Rican nationalist intellectual fed the Latino press. More and more blue buttons were being worn downtown. We were gaining momentum.

Conrad Worrill, our liaison with the Task Force, organized regular rallies and marches for Washington on the South Side, his beloved "base." The Heartland Cafe in Roger's Park was our northern outpost and Slim Coleman's newspaper had become a regular voice for the campaign. Lu Palmer had lost his radio show when Washington announced, but he continued to be a powerful voice in the black community.

A small network of progressives, mostly European Social Democrats, became key allies for events in the white working-class neighborhoods. Zalkin and I made sure Washington made regular stops on the Northwest and Southwest Sides, but the news media paid little attention to the events so far from the lakefront. I arranged a campaign stop for him at St. Gaul's church, 5500 S. Kedzie, in the heart of the Southwest Side. There was a crowd of some 200 nearby residents, mostly of Polish origin. Washington was late arriving, and I had to persuade him to leave the West Side where he was being greeted by cheering crowds.

But when he arrived he was eloquent, describing how he had grown up several miles directly east of there, and how his community and their community shared many of the same problems. The crowd gave him polite applause, but they were clearly impressed with his eloquence and his being so down-to-earth.

Zenobia and what you could call the civil rights wing of the campaign organized Women for Washington, Teachers for Washington, Students for Washington, and Lawyers for Washington. Moe worked on a platform for reform and good government.

On February 6th, the campaign held a giant rally at the University of Illinois Pavilion on the Near West Side. An enthusiastic crowd of 12,000, the largest rally for any candidate in the campaign, showed a joyous fervor as leaders from the black, white and Latino communities called for a new day in city politics.

The pavilion shook with cries of "We Want Harold! We Want Harold!" The rally felt like a religious revival, and in spirit it was a rebirth of Chicago's civil rights movement. Washington blasted Byrne as a "flunky of Ronald Reagan," and Daley as a ghost of the old machine.

We had shown the world this campaign was serious. For the first time Washington felt confident of victory. The man who orchestrated the whole rally, from planning to execution, was Sid Ordower, the producer of the weekly TV show "Jubilee Showcase," and a longtime civil rights and human rights activist.

But then, with only weeks to go, Al Raby decided he was going to take over campaign strategy. He named his own press secretary, and she was to lead our media efforts. She would come into the office in the morning and type up a press release, which was our media strategy of the day. We were no longer able to hold our press events. We were getting very little coverage.

We heard the new strategy group was meeting each night in the Hyde Park living room of Wayne Whalen, a leading lakefront liberal. I used the pretext of delivering documents to Raby one night and saw from the doorway some of the members sitting around a fire in the spacious living room. There was Raby, Whalen, Tom Coffey, Jacky Grimshaw, a black Hyde Park liberal, and her husband Bill, a professor at the University of Chicago. So these were the decision makers! This is where Zimmerman and Pat Cadell, the campaign pollster, reported.

An outsider might say this was a reasonable way to run a campaign, with such a high-powered strategy group. But the whole group was out of touch with the operation that had evolved, with battlefield promotions, into a very effective campaign.

Zalkin and I asked for a meeting with Raby, and the three of us had lunch the next day in a restaurant near the office. We told him the system wasn't working. We were no longer getting the media coverage we had been getting, and we could prove it. I had known Raby since the 60's when I was a reporter and he was the highly respected leader of the city's most important civil rights group: the Coordinating Council of Community Organizations. But he dismissed our concerns. He had confidence in his press aide.

The next day the press office went on strike. Washington, who was operating primarily out of his congressional office, sent his aide Clarence McClain to the downtown office to mediate. He called a staff meeting and demanded an explanation.

I presented the evidence that we were not getting newspaper coverage and said giving Raby's new aide control of media had thrown a wrench in the whole operation. Mark Zalkin argued that we were no longer coordinating with activist groups. David Potter, on loan from Illinois Bell, said the press office couldn't function.

McClain interviewed the other side and reported back to Washington that he didn't know who was right. I believe it was Ed Gardner who then sent in one of his bright young executives to settle the matter. He called a general meeting and hammered out an agreement. The press aide and I were both to head media, and if there were any disagreements Kari Moe would cast the deciding vote.

It was a victory for us. We didn't see the press aide again. We went back into full operation with two weeks to go.

A few days later Raby's whole operation was put on ice. Washington had heard that those meetings at Whalen's house included discussions of how he couldn't win (Cadell was no doubt reporting polls showing Byrne still substantially ahead) and how Raby should prepare for his own run for a congressional seat by making appearances on the South Side.

Washington wanted to fire him on the spot, but we advised him that it would not look good to fire a second campaign manager with weeks to go. So we simply operated without, and nominal control was given to the acting treasurer. In days Washington was back in touch with Raby, assigning him duties outside the day-to-day operation. Raby had been invaluable in moving the campaign downtown and setting up the basic structures, but he would no longer be part of Washington's inner circle.

The Final Push

Every morning we met in Washington's office with his secretary to set that day's final schedule, with Washington piped in from his apartment. Conrad Worrill came to those morning meetings and arranged marches and rallies in the black community. Worrill and his co-chair of the Task Force, Bob Starks, were academics and activists who were committed to the empowerment of the black community. They believed white institutions were keeping the black community enslaved, so I used to kid Worrill about working with a white man like me. But the Task Force planned and carried out remarkable events for Washington, like marches along the Robert Taylor Homes housing project, where they were greeted by cheering crowds.

We held a series of on-the-scene press conferences, such as when Washington supported protesters against a coal-burning electric plant that was polluting a Latino community. At the construction site of Presidential Towers, he demanded that it contain the subsidized apartments promised in the original HUD financing of the project. We planned these events in association with neighborhood and civic groups, and all were thoroughly researched. We were dominating the news. Mayor Byrne had her fancy TV ads, State's Attorney Richard M. Daley had some leading liberals and his part of the Democratic machine, but we had the news, we had the enthusiastic crowds. Every day it seemed there were more blue Washington buttons proudly worn downtown. We knew we were still down but we were gaining fast.

I had asked Washington if we could do an event about police brutality. He said we could, as long as I worked with Howard Saffold, the head of his security detail and longtime friend, and one of the founders of the Afro American Patrolman's League. Saffold put me in touch with the main organizations concerned with police brutality, and we staged a dramatic press conference in a downtown hotel.

Washington met privately with some 40 victims of police brutality, and then we opened it up to the press, with attorney Flint Taylor questioning witnesses in several cases of fatal shootings by police. Washington then vowed to establish a citizens' review board to conduct impartial investigations of police conduct.

After the press conference Washington strode over to me and said "Did you do this?" I thought he was praising the event so I started to list the key players. Then I saw that he was angry. He walked past me, controlling his fury. That shook me, because surely police brutality was a vital issue in the black community, and I had assumed he would take his usual bold stance. But clearly he had read my talking points before realizing what he was committing himself to.

In his mind we were baiting the police hierarchy and the Fraternal Order of Police, who were vehemently opposed to citizen review boards. It wasn't that he opposed the idea. He had worked with Renault Robinson more than a decade earlier to write legislation to create just such a citizen review board. But he had to make such important political decisions himself, not have them thrust on him by me or anyone else. In any case, it was a big story on TV that night and in the morning papers. It helped galvanize the black community.

The Thursday before the election, Washington was invited to a rally honoring a man who they said was shot and killed for wearing a Washington button. No one in thecampaign knew anything about it, and we in the press office were suspicious.

We checked the police report on the shooting, and it appeared that it may have been drug-related. We weren't sure, but thought there was a good chance the event was a trap. The location was in the Near-South Side territory of a street gang that had not shown support for Washington.

I told Washington it was too dangerous to go. He said he had to. People were outraged that the man had been shot for supporting him. How could he not go? So we agreed on a compromise. He would go, but we wouldn't tell the press. That night reporters kept calling to ask where Washington was. One reporter in particular, Paul Hogan from Channel 5, pressed me the hardest. Days before the election and Washington had nothing on the schedule? Where was he? I am not a good liar, but I did the best I could. "Maybe he's reading a book," I said. "You know he's a prolific reader."

In those final days we tried to use some non-verbal symbolism of diversity, such as Washington in the Asian community, or being blessed by his pastor. At a downtown rally we flew five flags: those of the United Nations, the United States, Illinois, Chicago and Black Liberation.

The final turning point in the campaign came that Sunday, when the papers reported how Alderman Ed Vrdolyak was trying to win over Daley voters to Byrne by fanning racist fears of a Washington victory. He didn't know reporters were present when he was giving instructions to precinct captains on the Northwest Side.

"A vote for Daley is a vote for Washington," Vrdolyak said. "It's a two person race. It would be the worst day in the history of Chicago if your candidate was not elected. It's a racial thing. Don't kid yourself. I'm calling on you to save your city, save your precinct. We are fighting to keep the city the way it is."

Vrdolyak was chairman of the Cook County Democratic Party and in charge of Byrne's ground troops. There was no escaping that this was Byrne's strategy, and the controversy consumed the news next two days. Washington cited Vrdolyak's "scurrilous racist statement" and demanded that Byrne "publicly denounce" him. She had no good answer.

Washington campaigned all election day Tuesday, then went to the McCormick Inn to await the results. An overflow crowd of supporters filled the ballroom. Speakers called it the rebirth of the civil rights movement and cited Dr. Martin Luther King's call in 1966 for a black mayor of Chicago.

We had prepared a list of some 20 speakers, but when it was Jesse Jackson's turn, number 16, he just kept on talking. Washington, watching with top aides in a room upstairs, was furious. Jackson had long been a polarizing figure in the city and had done little to help the campaign. Now, as the results were coming in and it looked like victory was assured, he was making himself the face of the campaign to TV watchers. But Washington still waited until he was certain he had won.

Finally, near 2 a.m., Washington went down to the ballroom to proclaim his victory. He grasped the microphone and firmly pushed Jackson aside. He stood smiling as the crowd roared a favorite chant, "We want Harold, we want Harold...."

"You want Harold?" he roared. "You got him."

In that acceptance speech Washington tried to allay the fears of white voters. "Our concern is to heal....I want to reach out my hand in friendship to every living soul in the city."

What a joyous night that was. A friend still calls it "Our Camelot."

The final figures were 36% for Washington, 34% for Byrne, and 30% for Daley. Washington won 85% of the black vote, but only some 5% of the white vote.

The downtown campaign had managed to run an acceptable campaign for the major media, but it was the Task Force's success in mobilizing the black community that made the difference. "We were the fire that heated the pot," was how Conrad Worrill put it.

A week later, Hogan called me again. He had found out where Washington had gone that Thursday night. "Reading a book, eh?"

Chapter 4

The General Election

Not What It Seemed

"So I told Uncle Chester: Don't worry," Mike Royko began his story the day after the primary election, "Harold Washington doesn't want to marry your sister."

Royko was by far the most popular columnist in Chicago, and his story that Thursday morning in the Sun-Times spoke directly to the fears of many on the Northwest and Southwest Sides as they saw that the Democratic candidate for mayor was a black man.

In their neighborhoods the battle had been between Mayor Jane Byrne and State's Attorney Richard Daley. It was a shock that long-shot candidate Washington had pulled such an upset. Royko was born and raised on the Northwest Side, and he understood their dismay. But he pointed out that Washington "is a smart, witty, politically savvy old pro."

At first everything went smoothly. There was a "unity luncheon," a friendly meeting with Byrne and Daley, where they both endorsed the primary winner. Ed Vrdolyak pledged the full support of the Cook County Democratic Party.

There was one small incident the night after the election when Washington and Mitchell were visiting the city's three main TV stations. At Channel 2, Washington reached out to shake the hand of anchorman and commentator Walter Jacobson, but Jacobson declined to take it. Washington and Mitchell exchanged knowing glances. But all in all there was still a celebratory feeling.

Washington made the rounds of leading business groups, assuring them of continuity on the city's major development projects. He named Dick Simpson, at the University of Illinois, and Bill Berry, the former head of Chicago Urban League, to head a blue ribbon transition committee to find the best of talent to head city agencies.

With a healthy 28 per cent lead in the early polls, and as the Democratic Party nominee in a heavily Democratic city, he was confident of victory in the general election just 7 weeks away. His opponent was a little-known former state legislator named Bernard Epton.

But then things started falling apart.

Several Democratic committeemen publicly endorsed Epton, and he had volunteers on the Northwest and Southwest sides clamoring to help his campaign. The National Republican Party saw there was a good chance for an upset and sent in their top strategist, John Deardourff, who unleashed a torrent of vicious attack ads. They all ended with the tag line: "Epton, before it's too late."

At the annual South Side Irish Parade March 13th, Epton was greeted like a conquering hero. They cheered wildly, as this wealthy Jewish Hyde Park businessman had suddenly become the Great White Hope.

Three days later Mayor Byrne announced she was reentering the race, no doubt inspired by the enthusiasm of those crowds. Democratic Chairman Vrydolyak immediately announced he would not support her write-in campaign. He was not about to let two white candidates split the vote again, and he had already established a working relationship with the Epton campaign. Of course he had to continue to give lip service to Washington.

Former supporter Teddy Kennedy flew in to ask Byrne to withdraw from the race and support Washington. But she kept on campaigning until, one week after her announcement, she was roundly booed at a Southwest Side retirement home. They did not want to see two white candidates split their votes once again. She withdrew the next day.

Meanwhile at the annual downtown St. Patrick's Day parade March 17th, Washington's lack of machine backing was on public display. Instead of leading the parade, as the Democratic candidate for mayor had always done, he was well back in the line, marching with Cook County Board President George Dunne, the man Vrdolyak had ousted to become party chairman. Dunne was to remain the only white committeeman in the city that Washington could rely on.

Washington lost the campaign's only debate March 21st. One factor was that Tom Coffey was not able to coach him, as he had done for the primary debates. In any case Washington was unprepared for Epton's attacks, which sneeringly exaggerated his jail time and license suspension.

Finally his scoffing remarks infuriated Washington. He lost control, launching into South- Side street talk that a white audience could hardly follow—something about taking off his shoes and throwing his dirty socks. It was a disaster.

Our campaign was clearly struggling. More and more committeemen openly endorsed Epton, and he was being greeted by huge crowds, especially on the Southwest Side. People who would normally be wary of a lakefront Jew were looking on him as the Great White Hope. "Go get em, Jew boy," some shouted. The hate literature was featured in the national press.

Part of the problem was that Vrdolyak, chairman of the Cook County Democratic Party, was giving Washington lip service, but working behind the scenes for the Republican Epton. An Epton staff member later said he called every day.

But also part of the problem was our own campaign. After the primary Washington decided he had to take more control. He was finally able to talk his congressional chief of staff, Bill Ware, into coming to Chicago to take over as campaign manager. He hired Grayson Mitchell, on leave of absence from the publisher of Ebony and Jet magazines, to be his new press secretary. I was named deputy press secretary.

In the heat of the primary battles, it had been white radicals and black nationalists who had played the key roles. In fact almost all the most important players, black and white, had been deeply affected by the killing of Black Panther leader Fred Hampton 14 years earlier.

Ware was leery of all of us. He came from a different tradition. A graduate of the University of Chicago Law School, he had held a top post at the American Civil Liberties Union before joining Washington's staff. Proper and cautious, he was a conservative liberal. He insisted on control of all campaign decisions, including Washington's daily schedule. There were no more morning meetings and only the occasional briefing packet.

Mitchell had been a top reporter at the Sun-Times and Newsweek, and was on good terms with all the different factions that made up Washington's coalition.

He had authority over all media relations, including the TV ads being worked on by Zimmerman and Cadell, who continued their meetings at Whalen's home with what came to be known as the "Honky Caucus."

Mitchell and I quickly formed a good working partnership, and we came to be known as the "salt and pepper twins." We agreed that Washington needed a white face to join his mostly black entourage on the campaign trail, so we hired Brian Boyer, another former Sun-Times reporter and a friend who had been my partner in publishing the short lived "Chicago Free Press." He soon became a trusted Washington aide, and his chief speechwriter.

We also agreed that Bill Ware was becoming a real problem for the campaign operation. The headquarters had been moved to offices in the South Loop. We still had Kari Moe in charge of the issues office, which was producing a detailed blueprint for proposed government reforms called The Washington Papers. Zenobia Black was still in charge of volunteers, and her index-card files grew to include 10,000 people, with some 30 coming in each day for mailings.

The problem was that there was no mechanism to include the different aspects of the campaign in event planning and scheduling. Both the Task Force operation on 47th street and the "Honky Caucus," still led by Al Raby, felt cut off from the mayor. Bill Ware alone was making the decisions, and he was exceedingly slow and methodical, traits that would soon earn him the title "Bottleneck Bill." But Mitchell slowly began to exert more influence, and the campaign started to get back on track.

Fighting Back

Washington was intrigued with how we had handled that Thursday night in the primary. He could make public appearances without the media knowing. He had me join him for three appearances that he preferred to keep quiet. I was there just in case a reporter did arrive. The first was a huge South Side meeting of Black Muslims. I was the only white man in a highly disciplined meeting of thousands. Of course Washington wanted to enlist the support of the Nation of Islam, but a history of anti-Semitic remarks from their leader, Louis Farrakhan, had made them anathema to the Jewish community. A second private meeting was with a group working for the independence of Puerto Rico, which was considered by some a dangerously radical organization. A third was at a gay bar in Boys Town. The lakefront liberals were pressuring him to support gay rights, but opposition was strong in the black community, especially among the clergy.

Zalkin had been put in charge of the campaign on the Northwest Side, and he worked closely with Mike Holewinski, a progressive former state legislator and member of Bill Berry's transition committee who had extensive neighborhood ties. The two arranged for Washington to attend services Palm Sunday at St. Pascal's on the Northwest Side. Walter Mondale was scheduled to be in town that day, and it could serve as a symbol of the Democratic Party's commitment to working-class ethnic neighborhoods.

Better still, Zalkin had connections to Polish progressives who could arrange for a phone call from Lech Walesa, leader of Poland's Solidarity Party, to demonstrate Washington's reform agenda for the city.

But Washington wasn't sure of the politics involved. After hearing my arguments, and the counterarguments by Dick Durham, a senior adviser, he asked the two of us to work it out.

We sat in the conference room and debated for over an hour. I had the utmost respect for Durham. A prolific author, he had been introduced to Mohammed Ali by Malcolm X in the early '60's and had co-authored Ali's biography, *"The Greatest; My Own Story."* He argued that the Polish immigrants in South Africa were the worst of racists, and that the overarching battle underway in the world was the struggle against European domination of third-world people. I argued that the call would bring Polish support and move the campaign away from race toward progressive policy.

I finally conceded that an endorsement by Walesa would not be well received by some of Washington's ardent nationalist supporters. He gave me a book to read.

But Washington and Mondale did go to St. Pascal's that Sunday and were greeted by an angry mob that had mostly been bussed in by a Republican strategist. Scenes of Washington and Mondale being booed and slandered by furious whites made national and international news. To my mind that phone call from Walesa would have humiliated the protesters. But as things stood, Chicago was becoming famous as a bastion of white racism.

Deardourff's strategy for Epton was to create a growing distrust of Washington, first with ad attacks and then by feeding the media a string of stories about his misdeeds, such as unpaid bills from past campaigns. An electric bill, a gas bill, leaked one at a time to provide new leads to the stories of Washington's negligence. Unpaid bills from past campaigns are commonplace, but it didn't sound that way in the papers.

Meanwhile Deardourff's ads dropped the tag line "Before it's too late" and presented Epton as a statesman with a good record on civil rights. Now that he had given voters emotional reasons to oppose Washington, he was ending by presenting Epton as a reasonable alternative.

With just ten days to go the Illinois Public Action Council released a report showing that Epton had received over $1.3 million in campaign contributions from the insurance industry while serving as the legislative expert on the subject. While not technically illegal, he had sold his seat to the industry, the group charged. This provided Washington with a new attack line against Epton, which he used with relish in a series of appearances along the goodgovernment minded lakefront. Bill Berry and Dick Simpson were finally able to gain Ware's approval for a press conference on impressive plans developed by his blue ribbon transition committee.

One afternoon, Washington and I happened to be walking across Daley Plaza after an event when he brought up the subject of the Shakman decree.

"Do I really have to sign that thing, Chris?" he asked.

"I'm afraid so. The liberals are really devoted to it, and some will turn on you if you don't go along. They're already shaky. We'll have to find ways to get around it."

He just kept scowling.

The suit had been filed by Michael Shakman in 1969, when Richard J. Daley was the all-powerful mayor and party chairman. It was aimed at some of the abuses of patronage, such as a carpenter being fired because he didn't carry his precinct. The suit won many court victories and a previous administration had agreed to not fire for political reasons. Washington agreed to sign the other half, which stated that people wouldn't be hired for political reasons. Sometimes reform ideas outlive their usefulness.

Why were the liberals pushing so hard to make him pledge to sign the Shakman Decree? Racism comes in many shades of gray. The decree would bar the hiring or firing of city employees for political reasons. What did that mean for a new administration taking over from the old Democratic machine? I guess it was insurance against Washington going wild. To us it looked more like handcuffs, and in fact it would come back to haunt us later.

The Final Push

With a week to go the Sun-Times broke a story that Washington was a slum landlord, with photos of his dilapidated apartment building, and cited some legal reason why he therefore could not serve as mayor.

I called Washington on the campaign trail and told him this was the most serious charge yet. We had to refute it fast. Washington canceled his appearances and went to his congressional office to dig out his records on the building. He and his brother had inherited the building and sold it five years earlier. He sent a messenger with the sale records to me at the downtown campaign office.

The packet arrived at 9:30 p.m. and I knew Channel 5 reporter Dick Kay was planning to focus on the slum landlord charge in his commentary on the ten o'clock news. I sent a volunteer to rush the papers to the station, and got a phone message through to Kay that he was about to receive sale documents. Just before air time he got the package. When it came time for his commentary, he began it as planned, but then switched gears. "If this document is what it appears to be, Washington sold the building five years ago," he said.

We disproved that story, but the Sun-Times never did do a retraction.

In the absolute low point of the campaign, Epton volunteers began passing out leaflets accusing Washington of being a child molester, and asking people to call the papers and demand to know why this fact was not being reported. The fliers used Washington's mug shot and what appeared to be the police report on his arrest. The news media were flooded with thousands of phone calls.

Zalkin was able to trace the leaflets to a Northwest Side Epton office, where a Vrdolyak aide had provided the supposed rap sheet, a combination of Washington's picture from his 1972 arrest and an unrelated police report.

We gave the evidence to Hogan, who did a full report that Wednesday night, stressing the fabrication by someone working for Vrdolyak.

That Thursday, five days before the election, Washington confronted the child molestation charges in what turned out to be the turning point of the campaign. He was outraged at the charge, and he vented his fury in a speech at Mundelein College that night. No one wrote any part of that speech for him. He was speaking from the heart.

With righteous indignation he pointed out that he had become something of a "folk hero" for children in the black community. And yet now he was being accused of child molestation! He waved the leaflet.

This assault on his character "is not going to be tolerated."

"Do you want this job so badly?" he asked of Epton. "Are you so singularly minded that you would try to destroy character? If that is the kind of man you are, and these are the kinds of dogs of racism and scurrilism that you are going to unleash, I say to you I will fight you day and night."

The two had known each other in the state legislature. "Bernie, how low will you go?" Washington demanded to know.

Epton had been called out, and his response was to virtually stop campaigning. There were five days to go before the election, yet he only made two or three more token appearances in safe locations. The momentum swung that night in Washington's favor.

Every Friday night there was a gathering of reporters, artists and political activists at Riccardo's, a restaurant and bar near the Sun-Times and Tribune buildings. That Friday evening I led an integrated group from the campaign to the bar in a show of force. We knew the flood of phone calls stirred by the child molestation leaflets had caused a state of anxiety in the city's newsrooms, but we were armed with the knowledge of the leaflets origins, and with Washington's bold challenge to Epton.

Mike Royko was there, huddled with Alderman Roman Pucinski, one of the Democratic committeemen publicly supporting Epton. So was one of the city's most respected liberal reformers, who I was startled to learn was now supporting Epton. He had been a friend for years, but that night we got into a heated argument that turned into an angry shouting match and a public spectacle.

How could he possibly be supporting Epton? I demanded to know. Because Epton had a good voting record on civil rights, he said. And because he was a moderate Republican who opposed the corrupt Democratic machine. I countered that Epton would be run by Vrdolyak, just like Jane Byrne had come to be, and he had stirred the worst forms of racist hatred. He countered that Washington was an irresponsible man who had run a totally inept campaign. Finally, cooler heads prevailed and we were separated. I like to think that our group's presence that night at least tempered what looked to us something like mass hysteria.

It was only later that I learned what had won over Epton's new converts. Pucinski was showing Royko and various leading liberals a fresh poll that had Epton with a comfortable lead. He was telling them to accept the inevitable.

Royko's Sunday column was headlined "If Washington loses, it will be his own fault." The column quoted my leading liberal friend as saying that Washington aides had rebuffed his offers to help straighten out the dysfunctional campaign.[23]

From Friday on Washington campaigned all day and night, with frequent stops in the white lakefront wards. He saw the crux of the campaign with a new clarity. Vrdolyak had been only pretending to give him support. The Democratic machine in all but a few white wards was actively supporting Epton.

Vrdolyak had decided he preferred Epton, who he could easily control with his majority in the City Council. Washington, with 16 black aldermen and several independents, would pose a real threat.

"Greed is involved in this campaign, profit is involved in this campaign, and they're using race to cover it up," Washington told cheering North Side rallies. It was a

---

[23] Florence Levinson's book, *Harold Washington: A Political Biography*, was published that summer and my liberal friend was quoted as saying it was "the most inept" large-scale campaign he had seen." She appears to agree with him despite my efforts at rebuttal. "This campaign was a remarkable achievement," Chandler adds, "the paid staff went from a half a dozen people at the beginning to 137 with 10,000 volunteers at the end. On election day every precinct in the city was covered. It was Harold's genius that kept the whole ship floating. He has an extraordinary ability to relate to all kinds of people" (274).

struggle within the Democratic Party between reform and the machine.

Meanwhile Epton was nowhere to be seen. He even missed a national news program Sunday morning devoted to the two candidates, leaving Washington alone to define the campaign. He was in great form.

That afternoon we received calls from the media asking for reaction to charges that a desperate Washington was using the race card in a last minute television ad called "Shame." I hadn't seen the ad so I asked for a description. Scenes from the civil rights movement and from the assassination of Dr. King, and then from the angry crowds at St. Pascal's. It asked voters not to cast a vote they would be ashamed of. I told reporters I'd get back to them within the hour.

This did not seem like a good idea to me. The way things stood we had excellent news coverage for the next day of Washington on network TV, proclaiming his battle against the machine, and greeted by roaring crowds on the lakefront. Epton hiding out. Stories on the ad would replace that news.

Besides, to my mind it sounded like "If you don't vote for Washington you are a hateful racist and maybe an assassin."

Bill Ware and I were almost alone in the office. He said he had not seen the ad nor given his approval. He called Mitchell at home. He had not authorized the ad either. Washington, out campaigning, said he knew nothing about it, and he was angry. The ad would probably backfire. Not a good idea to appeal to guilt.

He wanted to fire Zimmerman on the spot, but I advised Ware that we didn't want that to be the news for tomorrow either. Mitchell called the TV stations and canceled the ads. I called the reporters back within the hour, and the subject was not an issue in Monday's papers.

That morning Washington told reporters he had withdrawn the ad, which he blamed on an "amateurish" campaign.[24]

Zimmerman was very proud of that ad, calling it his best of the campaign. We heard that a member of the Honky Caucus had mortgaged his home to pay for the air time. The whole group loved that ad and really felt they were saving the campaign. Perhaps it would have helped, but I don't think so.[25]

I was finally able to reach Royko Monday morning. We had worked in the same county building press room some 20 years earlier and had been professional friends ever since. I argued that as of Washington's Thursday night calling out of Epton, the momentum was swinging in our direction.

---

[24] *Chicago Sun-Times*, April 12, 1983: 1.

[25] In his 2011 book, *Troublemaker,* Bill Zimmerman credits his commercials with turning the election. He called them "highly emotional TV spots that shamed Chicago for its racism....They caused a sensation" (413). In 2013, he coauthored an article claiming that the single ad "Shame" did the trick. Zimmerman fought for many good causes, but in this case he is mistaken. Of all the accounts of the campaign, only Kleppner's *Chicago Divided* even mentions the ad.

Epton was canceling appearances. It was the reformers against a Vrdolyak puppet.

Royko's column for Tuesday, the day of the election, was not exactly what I hoped for. "By kook or crook, we have to pick a mayor" was the headline. He said he was in the undecided column.

But actually he didn't mention Washington's jail time or Epton's brief hospital stays for depression. He argued with himself, and if you read it carefully he was harder on Epton.

The turnout that election day broke all kinds of records, with huge lines at polling places in the black community, united like never before since the assassination of Dr. Martin Luther King. Every level of black society, every union leader and minister and businessman and public housing resident and CTA driver was praying for their Harold to win.

There were also long lines of whites, especially on the Southwest side where many felt the election of Epton was crucial to the future of their communities. Epton was also doing very well in the lakefront wards.

Washington supporters gathered at Donnelly Hall that night to anxiously await the results. Everyone knew it was going to be close, and close it was. It wasn't until 1:30 a.m. that he finally entered the hall to the chants of "Harold, Harold." He had won 51.8 per cent of the vote.

"You want Harold, well here is Harold!" he said to joyous cheers. He gave a beautiful speech that night. As recorded by historian Paul Kleppner in *"Chicago Divided: the Making of a Black Mayor,"* he said:

"Out of the crucible of this city's most trying election...blacks, whites, Hispanics, Jews, gentiles, Protestants and Catholics of all stripes have joined hands to form a new Democratic coalition and begin in this place a new Democratic movement."

He made sure to reach out to Epton supporters. "I am mindful that there were many other friends and neighbors who were not a part of our campaign," he said, but now we must "heal the divisions that have plagued us," and "together we will overcome our problems."[26]

The key to Washington's victory was the amazing turnout in the black community, 85 per cent of registered voters. He gained 98 per cent of their votes.

Once again it was the Task Force, and the leadership of Conrad Worrill, Bob Starks, Lu Palmer and Richard Barnett that had done a beautiful job of uniting the whole black community.

The next major factor was the Hispanic vote, which went 85 per cent for Washington, up from 15 per cent in the primary. I don't know how he did it, but I do know he truly believed in the black-brown coalition, and made close

---

[26] Kleppner, *Chicago Divided,* 241.

alliances with progressive Latino political leaders such as Rudy Luzano, who lost a runoff election in Pilsen's 22nd ward by 17 votes. Luzano was murdered in his home weeks later in a case that was never solved. Washington continued his alliance with Luzano's campaign manager, Jesus Garcia.

In the Puerto Rican community he had the strong support of Jose "Cha Cha" Jimanez and the "Young Lords," a former street gang that had grown into a non-profit humanitarian organization. Jimanez and the Young Lords had been part of Fred Hampton's "Rainbow Coalition" in 1969.

We won just 12 per cent of the white vote. All the liberal lakefront wards went for Epton, and he was getting 99 per cent of record turnouts on the Southwest Side. But Washington got some 40 per cent in George Dunne's 42nd ward, and Slim Coleman's 46th.

I lived in the almost-all-white Northwest Side 47th ward, where Ed Kelly was the powerful committeeman and head of the patronage-rich Chicago Park District. He called his ward "the fighting 47th" and was a proud supporter of Epton. My son Chris Jr. was our precinct captain. We managed to get 18 per cent of the vote, and the Washington ward organization proudly made buttons proclaiming "The 18 per cent Solution."

Kleppner reports that pollsters for both Epton and Washington agree there was a surge for Washington among white voters at the end.

"While only a minority of the whites who decided in the final three days opted for Washington, those who did accounted for over a fifth (21.6 percent) of all his white voters."[27] It turned out most of those white votes lived in the all-white Northwest and Southwest Side wards.[28]

Travis puts it this way: "In the opinion of some political pundits, Harold Washington won his margin of victory during the last few days before the election when he put on his boxing gloves and came out in the middle of the ring fighting like Mike Tyson."[29]

---

[27] Kleppner, *Chicago Divided,* 235.

[28] "White Vote Key to Victory" was the front-page story in the SunTimes that Thursday.

[29] Travis, *The People's Mayor,* 195.

Photos by Paul Sequeira

The view from Cabrini Green

**Dr. Martin Luther King and Al Raby at the
Weston, Ill. open housing demonstration,
June, 1967.**

Dr. Martin Luther King

**Fred Hampton presides at a Black
Panther wedding, August, 1969**

**Fred Hampton's bedroom,
Dec. 4, 1969**

**Mayor Harold Washington faces
the press, November, 1986**

Washington and his fiancee, Mary Ella Smith

Robert Taylor Homes

Chapter 5

Council Wars

A Political Coup

The inauguration in the Grand Ballroom at Navy Pier was a sumptuous occasion, with Mayor Byrne and State's Attorney Richard Daley among the honored guests, and the 4,000 Washington supporters in the gilded hall, black white and brown, giving Washington a wild reception as he laid out his reform agenda. His friend Dempsey Travis devotes a beautiful chapter to the occasion in his book *"Harold, the People's Mayor."* Travis is at his best when he describes these kinds of public events.

The Roman Catholic Cardinal, a leading Rabbi and the Greek Orthodox Bishop all gave prayers, the Chicago Children's Choir sang and Pulitzer-Prize winners Gwendolyn Brooks and Studs Terkel read poetry. Travis records Washington's entire speech, in which he said he was inheriting a large deficit that would require immediate cuts, but his administration would lift "the burdens of mismanagement, unfairness and inequality...."

"I hope someday to be remembered by history as the mayor who cared about people and was above all fair, (extended applause), a mayor who helped to heal our wounds, who stood the watch while the city and its people answered the greatest challenge in more than a century --- and who saw that city renewed."

Three days later, on Monday, May 2nd, sixteen of us from the campaign moved into City Hall. It felt like a parachute landing. There was no pretense of transition. Byrne had just hired some 200 people to make sure there were no vacancies. Washington found a totally empty office. "Not so much as a paper clip," he noted.

Grayson Mitchell and I went to the press office and found some ten press aides in their cubicles and, thankfully, the main office and one cubicle empty. Some of the others had to fire someone to get a desk to work at. The newly appointed department head at Streets and Sanitation returned shaken to say he would need help in asserting any authority.

The City Council had scheduled a meeting for that morning. Washington met with his top council advisers, and was told he should adjourn the meeting. They were still negotiating with party regulars and freshmen aldermen.

He called the City Council meeting to order, recognized a motion to adjourn, and a second, called for a voice vote and gaveled the meeting to a close. He left the podium and twenty one aldermen walked out too. But only twenty one.

Vrdolyak was president *pro tem* of the old City Council, so he strode to the podium, called for a roll call on the motion, and he and his 28 allies proceeded to add committees, change committee chairmanships and pass ordinances restricting the powers of the mayor. He had carefully planned for this event, recruiting aldermen with new committee chairmanships, having the 29 swear a loyalty oath, and meeting for long hours with a whole team of lawyers to plan a legal takeover. It turned out that Chicago had a weak mayor system -- a majority of the city council was decisive.

It was a coup. Vrdolyak and Ed Burke, the Southwest Side alderman he named to head the all-powerful Finance Committee, would control the City Council for years to come, in what came to known as "Council Wars."

They blamed it all on a bumbling new mayor. First they said it was something Al Raby said days after the election, then it was the things Washington said about the machine in his inaugural address. Then it was James Houlihan, a state legislator that Washington had asked to help organize the council, who Vrdolyak claimed had threatened drastic measures. Burke was more blunt. "None of this would have happened had Harold come to us the way Byrne did."

The fact is that Washington had carefully crafted a moderate reform for the council. Vrdolyak's Building and Zoning Committee would be split in two, with Vrdolyak continuing to chair the Building portion. Fred Roti, the 1st ward alderman, considered a spokesman for the mob, would have to step down from the licensing committee, but would get another chairmanship. The idea was to reduce their influence but not humiliate them.

Days after the election he had met with Vrdolyak and Wilson Frost, the sitting black chairman of the all-powerful Finance Committee and a party regular. Washington told Vrdolyak that Frost would be his point man for the reorganization, and of his plan to split his committee. It was a gracious offer under the circumstances. But Vrdolyak rejected it out of hand, calling it an insult. Washington got angry.

"You supported Epton, bullshitted me, and you've been organizing since day one. Let's get it out front."

Vrdolyak responded he would not go down without a fight, and left the meeting. It's interesting that Gary Rivlin, in his generally first-rate book on the Washington years, *"Fire on the Prairie,"* doesn't believe what he reports Washington saying to Vrdolyak that day. He believes Vrdolyak's claim he simply didn't "break his back" for Washington. They didn't call him "Fast Eddie" for nothing.

Washington still fully expected to gain the support of the Daley aldermen, as they had no fondness for Vrdolyak, especially since he had won control over the Cook County Democratic Party from them the year before. George Dunne helped him arrange a meeting with the Daley forces, including Rep. Dan Rostenkowski, Rep. William Lipinski and Cook County Assessor Tom Hynes, and he offered to give the alderman from Daley's ward an important chairmanship.

The response was friendly but non-committal. He also asked Houlihan, a friend from his days in the state legislature, to help with the independents and the newly elected white aldermen.

Over the weekend before that first council meeting, Frost told Washington he thought they had 30 votes. It turned out they only had 21. Frost was blamed for the disaster of that first meeting. He had been outmaneuvered by the man they called "Fast Eddie." In the process the poor man also lost his chairmanship of the finance committee to Ed Burke.

You have to marvel at the way Vrdolyak orchestrated his takeover. The youngest son of Croatian tavern owners on the city's Far Southeast Side, near the steel mills, he was now the most powerful man in the city. Vrdolyak was a handsome, charming figure in tailored suits who had a flair for making things happen.

He had graduated from the University of Chicago Law School, and returned to the industrial Southeast Side to practice law. In time he was elected committeeman and then alderman of the 10th ward on an anti-bussing platform. He was involved in a number of questionable events over the years but always pointed that out he'd never been indicted. It was understood he had some connection to the mob. He remained the mayor's implacable foe throughout Council Wars, but even Washington came to think he was a likable villain.

The Press Wars

We held almost-daily press conferences those first few weeks to announce new cabinet appointments and executive orders and to give updates on Council Wars. His first appointment was of a new police chief. Mayor Byrne's chief had already announced he would resign if Washington was elected. Washington named Fred Rice, a high-ranking black commander who had the respect of the force. Washington was assuring white Chicago there would be no shift in law enforcement. It was also important to have the guys with the guns on your side.

For some reason Washington insisted to Mitchell that I accompany Rice to his swearing in. So we strolled over to the Daley Center from City Hall, making small talk, and he was sworn in without incident. I didn't know why Washington wanted me there. My white face? Did he expect trouble? To talk about police brutality? I thought he probably just wanted the swearing in to be carried out quietly.

The cabinet appointments Washington announced were very impressive: James Montgomery, the distinguished civil rights attorney, to be Corporation Counsel. Elizabeth Hollander, head of the Metropolitan Planning Council, to be Commissioner of Planning, Rob Mier, a specialist in community development at the University of Illinois, to be Commissioner of Economic Development. On and on, the best and the brightest. He kept Walter Knorr on as budget director, and hired back Sharon Gist Gilliam, a black financial expert fired by Jane Byrne, to assist him and take over after a transition.

Mike Holewinski reported directly to the mayor as liaison to the police and fire departments and to public transportation. Tom Coffey was soon placed in charge of dealing with the council as Head of Intergovernmental Affairs. Jane Ramsey, the Director of the Jewish Council on Urban Affairs, a successor to my father's Ecumenical Council, was made Director of Community Affairs.

Washington told Mitchell and Ware that the two of them were to run the government. He would handle the politics. He also wanted to resume the daily briefing packets, and Mitchell said that I would be responsible for producing them, as well as for participating in the scheduling meetings and joining him in reviewing Boyer's speeches. He would accompany Washington to important events and attend the strategy meetings with the mayor. We were to be the only spokesmen. We all were to address Washington as "Mr. Mayor."

On one of my first days in the office, the early edition of the Sun-Times carried a story about a secret meeting between Washington and Vrdolyak, at which the story said he "begged" Vrdolyak.

The story was written by Harry Golden Jr., the dean of the City Hall press room. He was the son of the famous author and brave reporter who challenged racial segregation in the South, but he had rebelled. He wore flashy clothes, loved the race track and would tell people the 29 were the good guys.

I knew Golden hadn't talked to the mayor, so he was just reciting what Vrdolyak had told him. I went down to the press room and confronted him about it. "The mayor does not beg," I told him. I knew where he had gotten his information.

In the next day's home edition the mayor did not "beg." He "groped." Thanks a lot Harry.

Over the next several weeks Golden gave such slanted coverage that I finally met with Ken Towers, the Sun-Times managing editor, and asked him to change reporters. He thought it was unethical of me to ask. I argued that all good newspapers rotate their City Hall reporters after one or two years. Golden had been there 15. He said he would do me a favor and not tell anyone I asked.

Meanwhile, we were losing the media wars. Almost everyone we fired filed a Shakman case, claiming they were improperly let go for political reasons. One expose claimed that Montgomery had hired someone with a criminal background (it turned out it was a courier given a second chance). Another one charged that Joe Gardner, head of the Neighborhoods Department, had once been arrested for having a gun (it turned out he had a permit and was working for a community organization in a high-crime area).

The newspapers delighted in displaying the supposed misdeeds of this so-called reform administration. Vrdolyak aide Joe Novak was expert at feeding the media his exposes. A regular taker was Michael Sneed, former Byrne press secretary who was now writing for the Tribune's Inc. column.

Our only friendly face in the press room was Chinta Straussberg, reporter for the black daily the Defender.

Washington called a meeting to discuss how we could improve relations with the media. When called upon I said "Well, if you wanted to make reporters happy, you could marry Mary Ella (his fiancee), buy a house in the old neighborhood and plant fruit trees in the back yard." Washington glared at me as if I was out of my mind and went on with the meeting.

Walter Jacobson charged one night in his Channel 2 News Commentary that Washington was lavishly refurbishing his Hyde Park apartment with city workers. He even had pictures of some workers there. It looked like the same old corruption to him.

We looked into it. The police department had decided he needed a more secure door for his apartment, and the workers had simply replaced the door. We gathered the documents and Mitchell and I met with Jacobson and some studio executives. We presented the documents and asked Jacobson to do a retraction. "I don't do retractions" he said. He advised us that if we wanted to balance things we should provide him with dirt on the Vrdolyak 29. But surely you have to set the record straight? He was not interested.

Fortunately Royko wrote a fine column about Jacobson a few days later, quoting his no retractions position and pointing out news organizations have a duty to set the record straight.

In those early days Washington tried to appeal directly to the liberal lakefront, bragging that he was going to end the evil patronage system once and for all. He even danced a little jig on the grave of patronage. I had to marvel at how well he threw himself into that act, since I knew his true feelings on the subject. But he had done as they asked, and signed the Shakman decree. He wanted to be rewarded for his sacrifice.

The Council Wars dragged on. Our lawsuit seeking to undo Vrdolyak's first-day coup was unsuccessful, leaving the balance of power in place. The 29 aldermen had a solid majority and voted down all of Washington's proposals, and kept in committee all of his appointments to boards and commissions. At the same time the 29 could not overcome a mayoral veto, which would have required a two-thirds vote. So there was a stalemate and little got done.

Black comedian Aaron Freeman coined the name "Council Wars" for his one man show based on "Star Wars," with Harold Skytalker and Lord Darth Vrdolyak. He spoofed both sides, which did not make it popular with Washington supporters. This battle was not about whites versus blacks, as the show implied.

Since the City Council was deadlocked, Washington issued a series of executive orders: opening up city records with a Freedom of Information Office, granting city employees the right to join unions, and directing police to not automatically turn the undocumented over to immigration authorities. These steps were largely ignored by the press, but each would have a major impact.

I remember buying the early editions of the Sunday papers every Saturday to see what new charge was being lodged against us. I would call the city desk and demand the right to respond. I was authorized to speak to the media, but on one story that summer I said something that caused Washington some political backlash (although I couldn't figure out why) so from then on I could only speak for the government. I referred political matters to Alderman Tim Evans, his floor leader.

Jesse Jackson had won a medal for negotiating the release of a Navy officer in Syria, and he asked if Washington would officially confer it on him in a ceremony at City Hall. But Washington did not want to be seen as too closely associated with Jackson, especially since he was now talking of running for president. Washington had his own slate of delegates for the nominating convention and didn't want to answer questions about who he was supporting.

The fact was he was determined to back Walter Mondale at the convention, when it could matter. It was crucial to defeat President Reagan. He asked Mitchell to minimize press coverage, so we made it simply a photo opportunity in the mayor's office. Jackson still spoke to reporters afterward, but he had little to say.

A special election was held in August to fill Washington's congressional seat. Lu Palmer entered the race and expected Washington's support, but Washington backed Charlie Hayes instead. Hayes was a longtime union leader and a good friend. Palmer and many of the activist nationalists were incensed; how could he turn his back after all Palmer had done to get him elected? Mitchell sounded me out on the subject and I said I understood that Washington chose Hayes because he didn't want to be so closely associated with an outspoken black nationalist. What I didn't understand was why he refused to talk to Palmer and did not assist him in any way.[30]

One morning Mitchell asked me to rush up to Clarence McClain's office. Tribune reporters were there and it looked they were going after him. I took the elevator up to his office and joined the interview in progress. Two grim Tribune reporters in suits were quizzing him. He was seated behind his large, cluttered desk, wearing his customary large thick-framed glasses and funny looking toupee.

The reporters asked him about his conviction for contributing to the delinquency of a minor. McClain said he managed a building where there had been a prostitution bust.

He went on to say the newspapers had claimed he was faking an injury from a car accident, and pulled his right leg up on his desk and showed them deep ugly wounds. I thought the reporters were going to faint, but McClain went on to demonstrate how he had to give himself two shots a day. He

---

[30] One of Washington's favorite soul food restaurants was Izola's on east 79th street, where he often dined with Hayes. Izola told me that one day Harold called her over to his regular table, where he was seated with Charlie, and announced that he was going to become the mayor of Chicago and Charlie here was going to replace him as congressman.

also managed to pull out the wad of bills he always carried in order to demonstrate some point. I really wished I had been able to talk to him beforehand.

The reporters, earnest young suburban men in ties, were obviously repelled by the sight of McClain's leg and were probably unaware of the fact that news reports had charged him with faking his injury. He had also been convicted of being the keeper of a house. McClain said it was only a $50 fine he didn't bother to contest. He said he was managing a building when police made a prostitution raid in one of the apartments. He tried to defend the women when he thought they were being mistreated and they charged him too.

In fact, McClain gave a very good defense of the two misdemeanor charges from many years ago. But the Tribune reporters seemed to be convinced they were dealing with an evil man and persisted.

Why had he not filed an ethics statement? They asked. "What ethics statement?"

I walked the reporters to the elevator, telling them McClain was a fine administrator who had a certain South-Side style. As we stood in the hallway waiting for the elevator I told them I hadn't filed an ethics statement either. I didn't think the new administration knew about the requirement. I was told later there was a debate in the Tribune city room about whether to include me in their expose of McClain.

And a big story it was. "Series of Vice Convictions Bared," the Tribune headlined. At that morning's press conference, Mitchell began by saying he hadn't filed an ethics statement himself. No one had. It was an oversight that would be remedied immediately. As for the other charges against McClain, they were only misdemeanors from over fifteen years ago.

The Tribune tracked down the victim in the "contributing to the delinquency" case, and flew him to Chicago from Michigan. They grilled him about the case at Tribune Tower, and were sorely disappointed to learn that he never met McClain. I don't think the Tribune ever reported that news.

But the press clamored for his resignation, and so did some of our liberal allies who had already considered McClain a dangerous liability. The fact was McClain was a first-rate administrator who Washington often depended on to get things done. Born and raised in the housing projects, McClain was a proud self-made man, a tool-and-die maker and skilled manager in a state job. He had insisted on earning $1 more than Chief of Staff Bill Ware. Washington was very reluctant to fire him.

He figured Vrdolyak must be behind the newspaper article, because McClain was his political negotiator with Vrdolyak. And in fact the story was broken by two reporters from the local paper in his ward. For Montgomery it was a case of an obvious smear of a very capable black man. Misdemeanors from fifteen years ago? Outrageous.

But Mitchell was adamant. It was nothing personal. McClain had been the one who talked him into joining the campaign. But keeping McClain would deal the administration a terrible blow. "The pawn has to be sacrificed to protect the king," he told them. Mitchell recalls that Washington cast him angry glances as he announced McClain's resignation. To him it felt more like he was sacrificing a knight.

Several times I asked Washington if we could take steps to encourage some public housing developments to become cooperatively-owned. The third time I brought up the subject he cut me off impatiently. "I don't want to hear another word on this, is that clear!" he ordered.

At one point that summer we received an offer from the mob. They could deliver four votes and bring about a 25 to 25 tie, with Washington casting the decisive vote. Only one of the alderman was publicly identified as being mob controlled. Tempting for a second, but no no no. Impossible. We are the reform administration. Besides, it may well have been a trap. Vrdolyak had his own ties.

But what a thought. Fred Roti and lakefront reformer Marty Oberman in the same caucus! We already had an unwieldy coalition that included black machine regulars only with us because of their constituents, and a few only kept in line by the threat of Task Force picketing.

This old guard included "Wild" Bill Henry, who wore big pinky rings and packed a gun even at City Council meetings; William Beavers, a former policeman who had open contempt for reformers; and Marian Humes, who Washington privately called "the snake with the golden tooth." She ran against Charlie Hayes in the election to succeed him in congress.

There were a few truly progressive black aldermen like Bobby Rush, former Black Panther leader, and Danny Davis, a civil rights advocate since Dr. King's Chicago campaign.

Tim Evans had been a sometimes maverick, but became an ardent believer in Washington's agenda and his floor leader at City Council meetings. Gene Sawyer was a quiet regular who supported Washington on a personal basis.

There were a few solid white lakefront liberals like David Orr and Larry Bloom, but Martin Oberman tried to distance himself as much as he could from the 21. Then there was Burt Natarus, out of place among reformers but George Dunne's alderman.

Somehow this unlikely coalition hung together, although there was resentment among some black aldermen that Washington was carrying out the liberal reform agenda by cutting staff, and anxiety among some white liberals about Washington's associates, especially Clarence McClain.

Meanwhile McClain was called a convicted felon and a child molester and a vicious pimp by Ed Burke and others in the 29. The news media repeated the charges while making no effort to set the record straight.

I thought the coverage was shameful. McClain was made out to be the devil incarnate.

The absolute low point came that fall when in the middle of a City Council meeting Vrdolyak made a request of the mayor by saying "To someone of your gender, I should say pretty please." Washington responded "You're about to get a mouthful of something you don't want, mister!"

"Is that a threat"? Ed Burke shouted. "If it is, come on down here!"

"You come up here!" Washington responded. The gallery was full of Washington supporters outraged at Vrdolyak's insult. Aldermen were threatening each other.

It looked like the two sides might come to blows, and I knew who I was fighting for.

Washington gaveled the meeting to a close. Shortly afterward he met with a group of angry supporters who wanted to take immediate action to avenge the insult.

He was able to calm them down, telling them that only political power would bring respect and directing them to mobilize for the next committeemen elections. Mitchell was impressed with Washington's skill in defusing the situation.

The white press didn't understand the anger in the black community at Vrdolyak's attack. Why were white people so afraid of a black man's sexuality? He had been called a child molester. McClain was accused of abusing minors. Now he was gay. How many insults did Harold have to endure?

Gaining Ground

And yet somehow Washington managed to get an ordinance passed quietly through the divided City Council that allowed city workers to join unions. His executive order had been challenged in court, and the judge ruled that an ordinance was necessary. Vrdolyak agreed to support the ordinance after a meeting with labor leaders who convinced him that was his wisest choice. Union organizer Henry Bayer says "Vrdolyak caved."

Bill Ware prepared a budget for 1984 that cut spending and contained economic reforms. But there were no initiatives, no new proposals. Washington gave the budget to Mitchell to fix, with just two days to go.

We had a meeting around Mitchell's conference table to figure out what traces of idealism we could add with a very limited budget. Mark Zalkin was there. I had lobbied to have him hired back from the campaign, and he was once again the mainstay for the daily briefing packet.

We looked up the reports and recommendations of the Bill Berry-Dick Simpson transition team and Kari Moe's Washington Papers, and we called for some of their recommended commissions and committees, including those on Latino Affairs and Asian Affairs, as well as a liaison to the gay community. We also included Zalkin's proposal to add a substantial number of public health nurses. The nurses who gave home care to pregnant women had been shown to reduce infant mortality rates.

Our changes were added to the budget, and Washington was pleased with our work. He asked Mitchell to prepare other progressive reforms for the government.

Mitchell called a planning conference for a Saturday afternoon, and we invited some of the most creative people we could think of. We invited John McKnight, Northwestern University professor and former Midwest Director of the U.S. Civil Rights Commission. Also Dick Durham, the author and former top adviser to Washington.

There were eight of us altogether, enjoying three hours of lively discussion. There were many fine proposals, but first and foremost was McKnight's suggestion that we establish a "Set-Aside" program for city contracts. We would establish a goal of twenty-five per cent of all contracts to be awarded to businesses owned by minorities, and five per cent to those owned by women. The city was to certify such companies and report annually on their success at meeting the goal. This would set up a mechanism to shift some of the city's purchasing power to the black and Latino communities.

Dick Durham suggested that we establish a "Welcome Baby!" program similar to the one they had in Cleveland. The idea was that whatever your background, you were welcomed with the finest care by the city.

Mitchell summarized our recommendations in a twelve-point plan and submitted it to the mayor. McKnight's Set-Aside program was immediately adopted. Mitchell came by my office to say "The mayor wants you to know he was already going to create that policy."

The mayor was emphatic about it, and it was true he was absolutely committed to getting the long short-changed black and Latino communities their share of city business, and Montgomery had already managed to shift some Corporation Counsel business to minority firms, but McKnight provided the outlines of a legal framework for a city-wide system.

The other proposals included a city beautification program, a student foreign exchange program, and a neighborhood revitalization project based on the "Nehemiah Project" in New York. None were ever acted on as far as we could tell. Mitchell's report lay on Ware's desk.

There was some tension between Mitchell and Ware, to be expected since the two shared power. Mitchell was incredulous when Ware canceled the Christian portion of the annual Christmas decorations at City Hall. There was a public outcry, but Ware insisted on the separation of church and state. Mitchell just couldn't figure out why Washington was such a believer in Ware. Sometimes Ware would even berate the mayor, and he would put up with it.

Washington clearly looked up to him intellectually. He had gone to the prestigious University of Chicago and its Law School. He could easily deal with white society, while Washington always felt unease. He was neat and organized, the kind of man who would never leave a bill unpaid. Washington was messy and sometimes distracted.

Ware was gay, but it was a closely guarded secret. So why, Mitchell wondered, was he seen taking his hairdresser to a fancy downtown restaurant? Mitchell somehow managed to squelch that gossip column item before it made print. Ware was not politically progressive. When someone presented a plan for new housing in Kenwood north of 47th street, Ware dismissed it out of hand. "Nobody wants to live there," he said.

On the other hand, Ware felt unfairly burdened when he was expected to carry out policies that Mitchell and I sometimes announced to the press in reaction to other stories. He was also especially antagonistic toward me. Mitchell asked me what I had done to him, but I couldn't think of anything.

But for all his faults, Washington could rely on Ware in a crucial area: there would not be even a hint of impropriety under his authority. We learned how important that was years later when a retired FBI agent told us that every phone on the 5th and 6th floors of City Hall was tapped from our first day in office. The mayor's office and Corporation Counsel were on the 5th floor, and the press office and intergovernmental affairs were on the 6th floor.

Gary Rivlin was a reporter for the Reader at the time, and his coverage in that independent weekly was much more balanced than the major media. His book *Fire on the Prairie,* is the most thorough examination of the Washington elections and administration.

But some of us in government made him nervous. In the book he is clearly disapproving of those he considered too radical.

"The good-government liberals...were never comfortable with the activists inside the administration – 'unprofessional' was among the kinder words they used to refer to these people who dressed in Hush Puppies, cheap sport coats, and out of date ties," he writes. "The technocrats were inclined to agree." I believe he is referring to me, Zalkin, probably labor activist Paul Waterhouse over at the new Freedom of Information Office, and Washington's friend David Cantor at the dangerous Streets and Sanitation department, and a few other friends in the administration. Later he refers to us as "protesters."

He describes Dr. Quentin Young, a former medical director at Cook County Hospital and one of the most respected voices on public health questions in liberal circles, simply as a "white lefty." Nowhere does he suggest that anyone might be right wing.

I partied a few times on the South Side, including late one night at the place-to-be for many of the most successful blacks in town, with politicians, judges, musicians, and many others on top of their game. There was music, cocktails, and excitement in conversation around the bar. What a celebration. I was told there was always such a place on the South Side, but the location changes often.

Another time we went to a dilapidated liquor store on 47th street, and at the back end of the store was a one-way mirror. We were admitted to a little jazz club, with an artist at the keyboard and folks dressed in their finest sipping cocktails. Elegant.

The Checkerboard Lounge on east 43rd street was still presenting the best in blues, and Teresa's, just south of Indiana on 47th, was still the place the big names came to play to a neighborhood crowd on Monday nights. But they were only the remnants of what was once the heart of the South Side.

Washington was born and raised in this neighborhood, called Bronzeville. In the 20s and 30s it was known as the jazz capital of the world. Dempsey Travis describes how for several years Harold, his dad Roy and brother Edward lived at 3936 S. Parkway (now Dr. Martin Luther King Drive), across the street from the Grand Terrace night club, home of the world-famous Earl Hines band. It was controlled by Al Capone, and like most of the other fancy clubs in the all- black area, it was for whites only.

Travis writes that "Young Harold spent many evenings looking out of his second-floor bedroom window at white women draped in mink coats and jackets and at white men in tuxedos, tails and top hats. They arrived at the door of the cabaret in their chauffeur-driven cars, eager to be entertained by Earl Hines and his all-star black orchestra and a jewel-studded colored floor show crowned with shapely mulatto girls."[31]

Washington was a lifelong admirer of his father, who started off working in the slaughterhouses, became a lawyer working for the Corporation Counsel, precinct captain and, by the time that he died, owner of several apartment

---

[31] Travis, *The People's Mayor,* 6.

buildings. Young Harold delivered newspapers and joined his father at political meetings and church services, where his father sometimes gave the sermon.

Roy Washington was one of the first blacks to switch allegiance to the Democratic Party when FDR was president. He worked long and hard for the party and when he finally won the Democratic nomination for 3rd ward alderman, he was sabotaged by his own committeeman, who supported the Republican opponent. Roy was bitter and his son shared that bitterness and vowed to succeed in politics.

Harold went to the nearby high school, Du Sable, where he was known as a bookworm and an athlete, winning the city high hurdles championship after careful study and training.

He married his high school girlfriend and then was drafted and served in a segregated army unit that built airstrips for our advancing armies in the Pacific. According to Dempsey Travis, he once served heroically as the only soil specialist for rapidly advancing forces, being flown from one frontline position to another.

On his own time he took correspondence courses and wrote for the unit newspaper. He was promoted to sergeant, but he always said he hated the army.

Back in Chicago, he and his wife had grown apart and were divorced. Taking advantage of the G.I. bill, he enrolled in the newly opened integrated Roosevelt University in downtown Chicago. He earned good grades and was elected head of the student council. He also actively supported early civil rights activities at Roosevelt, such as their right to eat at nearby restaurants. But he was careful not to be arrested or to join the more radical groups such as the Congress On Racial Equality (CORE).

He made many lifetime friends including Gus Savage, later a Chicago congressman, Dempsey Travis, a successful real estate entrepreneur, Bennett Johnson, onetime head of the Evanston NAACP and a publisher, writer Florence Levinson, and a number of other friends who had very successful careers.

He went on to get his law degree at Northwestern, where he was the only black in his class. After graduating, he took over his father's law office on 47th street, across the hall from Democratic committeeman Ralph Metcalfe, who had been a former Olympic champion. Washington had a succession of city jobs, first taking his father's place in the Corporation Counsel's office, then working as an arbiter for the Illinois Industrial Commission.

But his real energies were devoted to organizing the 3rd ward Young Democrats. Metcalfe's 3rd ward office was also on 47th street and was open every evening for drinks and discussion. In those days 47th street was the center of the South Side's political and cultural activity. Just down the street was The Palm Tavern, the black-owned business where the South-Side elite often dined, and the Regal Theater, the stately palace where Duke Ellington, Count

Basie, Louis Armstrong, Ella Fitzgerald, Sarah Vaughn, and Billie Holiday were regulars. Then there was the Metropolitan Theater, where the children watched double features on Saturday afternoons.

By all accounts Washington was a workaholic, spending endless hours discussing the craft of politics and building the 3rd ward Young Democrats into the most powerful voice for reform within the city's Democratic Party. They saw themselves as the cautious political arm of the civil rights movement.

Florence Levinson, who Washington dated at Roosevelt, describes what Washington was like in those days. "Talk, a game of chess, a book, a woman, and work, mostly work—that is Washington's life, the life of a serious man, but one with an endlessly buoyant sense of humor, not humor that is easily recorded, consisting as it does of a wink at the right moment, a phrase that relieves tension or makes light of something he wants to avoid, or a playful quip about an absurd situation. There's no Miller's joke book in Washington. He sees the absurdity of so much in life he cannot resist remarking on it, wryly, even slyly at times."[32]

He was a founder of the Negro Voters League in 1958 along with civil rights stalwart Timuel Black and Bennett Johnson, Washington's former classmate from Roosevelt and frequent political collaborator. But Washington cautiously kept his name off all of the paperwork.

---

[32] Florence Levinson, *Harold Washington: A Political Biography*, 77.

In 1965, when there was an unexpected opening for the state legislature, he was slated with the help of Metcalfe and, from the outside, pressure from members of the Negro Voters League.

In his first year he was named Legislator of the Year by the Independent Voters of Illinois, but then the Democratic machine clamped down, and for many years to come he was forced to vote most of the time according to the "idiot sheets" provided by the party. He had to choose his issues very carefully and there was evidence he was under great strain.

But over the years he rose to state senator and then congressman, expanding his base of support with regular weekend campaigning. As a congressman, Washington represented Chicago's lst Congressional District, which had been represented by black men for longer than any other district in the country. It was still a vibrant community, even though the largest public housing project in the country, Robert Taylor Homes, now lined its western border, aimed at confining any expansion.

More Dirty Tricks

Washington supported Larry Bloom when he challenged Richard M. Daley in the Democratic primary for State's Attorney, slated for March 20, 1984. The 29 backed Daley and unleashed vicious attacks against Bloom. They claimed the child molester Clarence McClain was in his campaign.

"When the Washington Bloom McClain political caravan comes around to your neighborhood," Burke said in a radio interview, "the mothers and fathers of Chicago children better lock them up and keep them out of the way." Burke went on to claim McClain beat his prostitutes with coat hangers. Bloom lost the race badly. Washington considered Burke a dangerous racist.

That spring I had a private conversation with Washington about Council Wars. I proposed that I reach out to a member of the Daley faction and see if we could win some votes to our side. Washington told me to go ahead and give it a try, but not to tell anyone.

I called congressman Lipinski, and we arranged a meeting in his office. I was still driving the city car, so that Saturday I took buses to Lipinski's Southwest-Side headquarters, gave a false name and was ushered into his small office at the end of the building. He asked his aide to shut the door, and we began to discuss possibilities.

He said we could receive some aldermanic support if we would support some of their projects. As a test case we could start off with a proposal pending approval for a new playground in Michael Sheahan's ward. I told him that sounded like a worthy project, and we should be able to gain approval soon.

At the end he admonished me that I could not delegate any authority. They would deal with me only. I responded that it had to be that way since I was a back channel to the mayor.

So I waited for a casual opportunity to talk to Washington. That was a terrible mistake. That Tuesday morning I got a call from Ware, and he was irate. Sheahan had asked him what was holding up the approval. He gave me a tongue-lashing for a good five minutes.

Mitchell came by my office, bemused by the situation. Ware had chewed me out? I should have seen Ware's rage at the mayor. He treated him like a naughty child, Mitchell said.

Wasn't Ware interested in breaking the impasse of Council Wars? Not if it was through me, he wasn't. He was opposed to that kind of political horse-trading anyway, although he would have accepted it from the mayor. I blamed Sheahan for the disaster: I was supposed to be the sole contact. But I blamed myself the most for not contacting Washington right away.

Mitchell hired a new press aide who spent her full-time interesting the media in profiles of new commissioners, especially the women, and of the people appointed to boards who were blocked by the 29. Rob Mier had revamped the Economic Development Department, with the help of Kari Moe, and there were positive stories in the press about his efforts to steer development funds to community organizations. The media seemed to be running short of exposes of our wrongdoing. Editorials appeared urging the Vrdolyak 29 to release Washington's appointments. We were slowly gaining acceptance.

That summer Vrdolyak held a press conference in front of a pile of trash on the Near Northwest Side. The Washington administration was so inept it wasn't even able to take care of garbage in the streets, he said, hinting at the possibility he might run for mayor.

Zalkin found out the owner of a nearby business had witnessed a strange sight that morning. A city garbage truck had cleared out an ally, and a half hour later another city truck arrived and dumped its contents. A little later Vrdolyak had held his press conference in front of the fresh trash.

What a story! Vrdolyak had to bring in trash to accuse the city of ineptitude. I put Paul Hogan in touch with the businessman, and Hogan prepared a scathing story. Vrdolyak would be the laughingstock of the whole city.

But then Ware got wind of it, and I was called to a meeting in the mayor's office. Unfortunately Mitchell was on vacation. I laid out the sequence of events for the mayor and ended by saying that Hogan would ridicule Vrdolyak on Channel 5 that night.

Ware insisted that we had to hold a press conference. Someone had allowed Vrdolyak to commandeer a city truck. We should investigate and punish those responsible. But I was adamant that we should let Hogan break the story. People would be laughing at Vrdolyak. Washington could not decide, so he asked me, Ware and Brian Boyer to go into the conference room and work it out. Much to my dismay Boyer sided with Ware.

When we first hired him I had told Boyer that he had to remain loyal to me in a very tricky political climate. Now he was siding with Ware. Apparently he was currying favor in hopes of replacing Mitchell as press secretary. In any case, I gave him the contact information for the businessman witness, and he helped Ware with his press conference that afternoon.

Then we got word that something had gone wrong. I drove out to the businessman's office and passed Vrdolyak and his aide Novak as they left. They waved happily. It turned out the businessman's mother was now denying the whole story. She had been there all morning and saw no trash being picked up or dumped. Vrdolyak was such a clever man.

Hogan caught the businessman at the airport just before he left town. He laughed off the whole crazy situation. He saw one thing and apparently his mother saw another.

A few days later Mike Royko salvaged some of the story. He quoted the businessman describing how he watched a garbage truck dump trash in the clean lot, and city workers spread it around before Vrdolyak held his press conference.

The argument over how to handle that story was symptomatic of a power struggle under way that summer. Mitchell believed that Ware's disease was beginning to affect his judgment. He would come up to Mitchell's office, get angry and sound incoherent. Mitchell believed he was determined to get us out of the mayor's office before he died, partly because he was afraid we would not keep his AIDS a secret. We and several others believed he was becoming unstable, and should be replaced by Corporation Council James Montgomery. Montgomery was a good administrator, and was being widely praised for bringing professionalism to the Corporation Counsel's office while at the same time increasing minority representation.

So there was a quiet war going on within the administration. Slim Coleman came to my office that summer and tried to talk me into supporting Ware. I pointed out that Ware appeared to be having difficulties with his health and that Montgomery clearly had the best management skills. Coleman denounced Montgomery as a middle-class, middle-of-the-roader. I said Ware was a reactionary. The conversation got heated and I ended up telling Coleman that he was only supporting Ware because he must have just received some grants for his organization. He stormed out of the office.

Washington looked bad at that summer's Democratic National Convention. It made network news when he was shouting to turn off the camera. The correspondent had been interviewing Washington about how his delegation was going to vote, when Vrdolyak appeared, so the correspondent then asked the mayor if he and Vrdolyak would discuss Council Wars. Washington blew up. Probably there was nothing that could have been done, but Mitchell and I thought Washington made a mistake by bringing only Boyer with him for press at the convention.

That fall I drove my oldest son to start college at DePauw University in Indiana. A family member, angry with me, wrote a letter to Vrdolyak saying I had used a city care for personal business. As it happened, the letter went to Dennis Church, an able former press aide who had defected to Vrdolyak. He called to tell me that he had filed the letter in the waste basket. I told him I almost forgave him for going over to the dark side.[33]

Finally, Washington decided to draw a line in the sand with the Vrdolyak 29. They could not muster 32 votes to overcome his veto. He would veto approval of a multimillion-dollar O'Hare expansion until they provided him some leeway on city contracts. As part of their coup after the election they had passed an ordinance that most contracts had to be approved by the city council. Washington would not budge until that was changed so that only contracts over $100,000 required approval.

Washington had used similar tactics in the state legislature, choosing the times when legislation could be delayed until he was able to force approval of his agenda. He vetoed the O'Hare ordinance, and called a rare general meeting to discuss ways to bring pressure on the 29 to concede. I suggested we arrange for a full-page ad by some of the city's leading businessmen demanding that the 29 let the O'Hare contracts move forward. Their opposition to the

---

[33] In the early days I had been given the unmarked police car and ran some emergency missions, such as leading Walter Mondale's motorcade from O'Hare airport to a press event at the steel mills, siren blazing. When Zalkin joined us in the press office, I drove him to and from work every day. He had multiple sclerosis that made walking difficult.

mayor was hurting the city's future. I also suggested a lawsuit against the 29 charging they were costing the city jobs and future growth. Among other steps, Washington assigned someone else to bring about the ad, and I was to arrange for the lawsuit.

I called Flint Taylor, the highly respected civil rights lawyer, and he agreed to prepare a suit. A few days later I was summoned to the mayor's office. Montgomery was there, outraged that I had asked Taylor to file the suit. He was a radical and would present the wrong impression to the public. Washington asked for my response, and I backed off. It was fine with me if Montgomery had found a more suitable lawyer. I had only asked Taylor because he was the only attorney I knew well enough. The following week the suit was filed and the full-page ad appeared.

Washington won that battle. The 29 agreed to his terms, and for the first time since he was elected he had gained some measure of power.

A few days later Mitchell returned from a meeting with the mayor and called me into his office. He said he had good news and bad. The good news was that Harold said he has won Council Wars. A federal lawsuit charging discrimination in the drawing of ward boundaries was going well. He was assured of special elections that would make it possible to gain control of the city council. That, and his newly gained control over city contracts, meant victory was in sight.

The bad news? "He says he doesn't need us anymore."

We were gone within two months.

Chapter 6

After We Left

Washington Wins

I have to admit Washington was right. He didn't need us. He went on to win reelection in 1987, beating Jane Byrne in the primary and Ed Vrdolyak in the general. He now had a solid majority in the City Council, and that summer he took over control of the Cook County Democratic Party with his ally George Dunne. He had become very powerful.

He was recognized as a hero overseas, sometimes greeted with cries of "Harold." He was a black man who had formed a rainbow coalition to win power and overcome bigotry. A big, dignified but friendly leader who stood for fairness. Washington had achieved his highest ambitions.

He was gaining some national prominence through the U.S. Conference of Mayors, where he was proposing a National Urban Agenda that would counter some of the draconian cuts in aid to cities that were being carried out by the Reagan administration. It included a $25 billion fund to rehabilitate the country's public housing buildings.

But some of us felt that he had moved too far to the center. His budgets trimmed waste and he took bold steps for open government and ethics enforcement, as Dick Simpson describes in the chapter on Council Wars in his *"Rogues, Rebels and Rubber Stamps."* The mayor pleased the lakefront liberals and newspaper editorial writers, but his government did not do as well on issues raised in that first campaign, like public health, or education.

That was largely because the government bureaucracy had become cautious and defensive. Bill Ware had won. Even as he was dying of AIDS in the Sloan Kettering Clinic in New York, he carried out a reshaping of the government through his successor-to-be, Earnest Barefield, who came from Philadelphia with a reputation as a careful administrator. By the time he died in May, Ware had replaced many aides, including Mitchell with Alton Miller, and me with Gladys Lindsay.

They were still the salt and pepper twins. Lindsay had handled press at the police department, but Miller seemed an unusual choice, coming from a ballet company. Mitchell didn't want to have anything to do with him, but I showed him how the office worked. You could make a case that presenting fresh faces to the media might help improve their attitude. Miller was kind enough to say I was "enormously helpful" in the transition.[34]

---

[34] In *Harold Washington: The Mayor, the Man,* Miller notes that I "was indispensable to the operation of the office during my first week or so." Alton also tried to explain the politics. "He had been a supporter of Harold Washington since before the campaign, a veteran newsman, respected in both political and journalistic circles. He had put himself-or had been put--on the wrong side of the internal struggles, and was being swept out by the same broom that was sweeping me in" (45).

On Miller's first day, what looked like a big scandal appeared on the front page of the Tribune. Washington had been caught by a secret tape-recording trying to bribe a candidate out of an aldermanic race,   as well as viciously attacking the candidate he backed, according to the story by gossip columnist Michael Sneed. Montgomery immediately called a press conference to denounce the taping as illegal under Illinois law.

The recording was made by James "Skip" Burrell, a longtime machine regular who was running in the 3rd ward against Dorothy Tillman, a civil rights activist who had first come to Chicago as part of Dr. King's advance team in 1965. Washington had appointed her to complete the term of the alderman who was serving time for accepting bribes, and was now supporting her election. Burrell thought Washington might threaten to fire him, since he was a city worker. Longtime Washington aide Sam Patch had failed to talk Burrell into dropping out and so had invited him to meet with the mayor as a last resort.

The Tribune revealed that the tape had been provided by the Vrdolyak camp, and Montgomery labelled the taping "Vrdolygate," which became the headline in the next day's Sun-Times. Washington and Tillman walked arm in arm to that day's City Council meeting, demonstrating that there was no rift caused by the tape. Tillman told the press "Dr. Martin Luther King taught me in the movement that white folks have always worked overtime in dividing Black people for their own welfare and with no regard for ours."

But the real game changer came when the Tribune published the entire transcript of the tape that morning. It turned out that Sneed's initial charges were grossly misleading. Yes, Washington had been critical of Tillman, but he also praised her. Washington had not tried to bribe Burrell out of the race. He had tried to win him over to his team, offering to support him if he ran the following year for state representative. Tillman would reimburse him for any campaign expenses he had incurred, and support him in the state race.

Ironically, the tape did more to gain the trust of the white public than anything else Washington had done. Padding around his apartment, cooking breakfast and chatting with a longtime acquaintance on the other side of Council Wars, the worst thing he did was swear a lot. No threats. No bossism. Only a crafty mayor trying to win an opponent over to his side. He flatters Burrell and disparages Tillman, but then notes that she has done as well as any new alderman, and ran a highly successful ward cleanup program.

"Look at the situation," he says. "She represents a coterie of activist people. Not just in the 3rd ward, which she doesn't control. She is just part of it. She represents that group. And that group has been helpful to me."

When Burrell presses him again and again about why he was transferred in his city job, Washington finally snaps "Well, don't saddle me with it. I got more things to do than fuck with you." Washington also corrects himself when he says "girls" when he meant to say "women."

The Vrdolyak camp's dirty trick had backfired. Burrell stayed on the ballot, and Tillman won in a landslide.

Three weeks earlier the newly hired Barefield had called me to a meeting to fire me. I told him he couldn't do that. It would have to be the mayor. Two weeks later I was called into Washington's office. He was as cold as ice. I reminded him I'd worked for him since the primary and said I would like to fill the vacancy of Director of Public Information at the library. He reluctantly, even angrily, agreed.

So I went to the library in March 1985. Mitchell started his own consulting company, and Boyer, who had just been fired for taping an ad at City Hall without permission, returned to his own video company. Boyer had been considered for press secretary, but Ware insisted he be fired for this supposedly serious ethical violation. Ware wanted his own man. It would be best if it was someone no one knew, hired by resume, in accordance with his version of liberalism.

In another year Corporation Counsel Montgomery was replaced by Judson Miner, a leading independent attorney, and Tom Coffey, Head of Governmental Affairs, was replaced by Jacky Grimshaw. At the time we blamed our firing on Ware, but when Montgomery and Coffey were replaced the next year it became more clear that the order must have come from Washington himself.

Simpson, who was a key adviser to Washington at the time, describes how Washington managed to achieve major changes in the government despite the deadlocked City Council.

"Unlike Byrne, Washington brought a broader based 'rainbow coalition' to power by his appointments. He promoted progressive whites, Latinos, and women, as well as blacks, to top positions in city government. Smaller groups like Asians and homosexuals also received posts in government and had their concerns addressed.

"Many city agencies were more effective and more responsive to neighborhood organizations than before. Federal government funds for social services and Community Development Block Grant money were no longer used primarily to hire patronage workers but returned over to churches, social service agencies, and community organizations to deliver social services more cheaply and effectively."

Simpson also details how Washington ended a protracted battle over the allocation of $126 million in federal Community Development Block Grant funds by proposing a $110 million city bond issue for neighborhood improvements. The Vrdolyak 29 responded by raising the amount to $185 million and the result was rare peace in the city council.

Simpson notes, "The planning department produced a series of maps showing how money from all sources

(CDBG, the bonds, city and state funds) produced the most even distribution of spending for neighborhood improvement in Chicago's history. Every ward, including the white ones hostile to Washington, shared equitably in the funds."

In early 1986 Washington withstood a federal undercover investigation that targeted four black alderman and Clarence McClain. That investigation, by an undercover mole with a long criminal background, smacked of the FBI tactics of the Nixon era. McClain was convicted of conspiring to get a contract approved at City Hall, even though his client didn't get the contract. Four alderman were convicted of taking payoffs, including Marian Humes. But neither the mayor nor any of his top aides were implicated.

The one member of the administration caught in what the FBI called "Operation Incubator" was John Adams, a deputy director in the Department of Revenue, who had accepted a $10,000 "loan" from the FBI mole, Michael Raymond. On a scale of one to ten, columnist Mike Royko rated the operation a two, and the charge against Adams a three. "It's almost embarrassing to think of this as a true Chicago scandal," Royko wrote, noting that veteran politicians could take in more in a single week.

In May 1986, 15 months after we left, the first special aldermanic elections were held as a result of the discrimination lawsuit, and four new Washington supporters were elected, giving him control of the City Council.

Council Wars was finally over. He had defeated Vrdolyak. His appointments to boards and commissions were finally approved. He was able to pass an ethics ordinance and a tenant's bill of rights.

Many good people continued to do good work for the mayor. Kari Moe was deputy director of the Department of Economic Development, which did important work in redirecting development money from downtown to the areas of need, and supported neighborhood organizations.

She and Rob Meier, the Economic Development Commissioner, worked closely with John McKnight's group at Northwestern University to provide neighborhood organizations with regular reports from the city on building code violations and police arrests in their areas. Their work set in motion what was to become the Chicago Alternative Policing Strategy, or CAPS.

Kari Moe then became assistant to the mayor in charge of economic development and several other departments. Holewinski was assistant to the mayor in charge of police and fire and transportation, and succeeded in breaking up the monopolies of the cab companies and increasing the number of driver-owned cabs. Zenobia Black was in charge of the homeless program at the Department of Housing, and helped create a network of shelters across the city. Zalkin was still the mainstay of the daily briefing packet.

At the Library

I spent a year at the library, which was still being run by Jane Byrne appointees. I never did meet the commissioner, and I was in Siberia as far as City Hall was concerned. But I enjoyed working with the senior librarians. I ran a book amnesty program for them and was given a weekly author interview radio show that I really enjoyed.

Vartan Gregorian, head of the New York City library, visited Chicago that summer to speak at a conference. He urged us to follow their example by appointing a whole new library board of prestigious figures from the universities, the church and the literary world, giving it new authority and initiative to strive for excellence. Inspired by his talk, I quietly and unofficially lined up an impressive new board, and passed the suggestion on to my City Hall liaison. A few weeks later I heard back: the chief of staff was not interested in a new board.

That fall I was helping to design a section of the new library devoted to news from around the world, with live feeds from each continent via satellite, newspapers and magazines from each, and regional experts to assist with questions.

Then I was caught running a mission for City Hall, and was fired. Kari Moe was my liaison to the mayor, but since Washington had not been able to name his own people to the library board it was still being run by Byrne appointees. In November 1985 the board was planning to hire John B. Duff, the chancellor of the Massachusetts Board of Regents of Higher Education, to be the new commissioner, but two black commissioners backed the assistant city library commissioner from Los Angeles, who they argued was more qualified. Kari asked me to plant a story that Washington had doubts about Duff. I planted the story at the Tribune, which quoted anonymous sources.

A few days later, board member Tom Rosenberg called me. He had been able to pressure the Tribune reporter into telling him the source of the story. Why did I tell the reporter Washington had doubts, he demanded to know. He reminded me that I worked for the board. Who told me that Washington had doubts? I tried to be evasive but he said he would bring me before a public board meeting if I didn't tell him. So I told him it was Kari Moe. When I told Kari she was very upset I'd identified her, and rightly so. I should have put Rosenberg off and consulted on what to do, but I failed to handle the situation correctly, and exposed her. In any case, Rosenberg had traced the report to the mayor's office.

Duff was confirmed by a five to two vote, with the black chairman, James Lowry, voting with the majority for the sake of peace. Duff took office and fired me, giving me three months to find another job. I applied to teach journalism at Northwestern. I was chosen by the selection committee, but the dean vetoed me. The head of the selection committee, Professor David Protess, resigned from the committee in protest. I became a freelance writer.

The Final Months

When Washington ran for reelection in 1987, he still had the backing of Slim Coleman, with his network of activists, and his partner, fellow activist Helen Shiller, who had designed the original campaign buttons. She had just been elected alderman and was one of his strongest supporters. He still had Conrad Worrill and Bob Starks and their somewhat weakened Task Force. He still had the solid support of other progressives like Katy Hogan and Mike James at the Heartland Cafe.

He ran what we thought were lackluster campaigns against Byrne in the primary and Vrdolyak in the general. He hired David Axelrod as his media director. Axelrod had covered the 1983 campaign for the Tribune, then quit to become a media consultant. He was hired as the media director for the senate campaign of Paul Simon and was promoted to campaign manager. Don Rose was also retained.

But for all this expertise Washington seemed defensive and uninspired. He beat Byrne with just 54 per cent of the vote, and faced in the general election Vrdolyak and Tom Hynes, the Daley block's candidate, both of whom were running as third party candidates.

Washington was pleased to be facing two white candidates, but when Hynes dropped out of the race with days to go he became concerned. Vrdolyak had won the candidate debate by a wide margin, and Washington was bitter toward his campaign staff for stifling him, as his press secretary Alton Miller relates in *"Harold Washington; the Mayor, the Man."*

"The mayor threw away the campaign organization's consensus schedule and asked Ed Hamb (his scheduler) and me to set up the final days for him," Miller writes. The three of them met at a soul food restaurant to plan it out. "The mayor was a whirlwind, and Ed was reminded of the frenetic pace of the 1983 campaign."[35]

Washington won, once again receiving just 54 per cent.

He was now winning City Council votes with margins of 39 to 11. Among the new arrivals were Helen Shiller, and Jesus "Chuy" Garcia, a community organizer from Pilsen who had been Rudy Lozano's campaign manager and who Washington considered his most able young politician. Also elected with Washington's support was Miguel del Valle, who became the first Latino in the Illinois Senate.

Vrdolyak, his longtime foe, had to resign as Democratic Party chairman, and Washington's trusted ally George Dunne regained the chairmanship. He was gaining national prominence as a force to be reckoned with.

That fall an editor at the Sun-Times asked me to write an assessment of the Washington administration for the Sunday commentary section. That article, which they

---

[35] Miller, *The Mayor, The Man,* 304.

headlined "Get moving Mr. Mayor," was an angry attack on the lack of progress made on some of the main issues of the first campaign, like education and public housing and police brutality.

Washington had refused to get involved in the teacher strike that fall, leading a group of parents to chant outside City Hall: "We Want Harold."

Dr. Jorge Prietro, head of the Chicago Board of Health, had publicly criticized the administration for letting infant mortality rates increase in the city. He was a Washington appointee and a man of almost legendary stature in the Latino community for his efforts to serve the poor. The administration's response was to evade the question.

My article began with Dr. Prietro and ended with Dick Durham's call for a "Welcome Baby!" program. In between, I described the cumbersome bureaucracy of chief of staff Earnest Barefield, who turned out to be more of a bottleneck than "Bottleneck Bill." There was the disaster at CHA, where Renault Robinson had battled the sometimes corrupt companies and unions serving public housing, only making things worse. The mayor had stayed away from the teachers' strike and done little to curb police excess.

I called Mitchell a few days later and asked him if Washington had seen the story. "Seen it? The whole South Side is talking about it. Harold is furious."[36]

------

[36] I came to realize while working on this book that Washington had given me opportunities to act on the issues that mattered most to me, and

I saw the mayor a few weeks later, at a big farewell party for Sun-Times reporter Basil Talbott, who was being assigned to the Washington D.C. Bureau. Washington saw me from across the room, but we didn't talk. What would I have said?

Five weeks after the article ran he died, and I felt terrible. I had just been called out of town because my father was dying. When I arrived at our farm in New Hampshire there were urgent messages from the media asking for comment on the mayor's death.

They said he had died of a heart attack while meeting with Alton Miller. I told them it was untimely, as he had just obtained his full powers. We would never know what he might have accomplished.

My father recovered and I flew back to Chicago still feeling guilty that my article might have contributed to his death. I called Mitchell and told him how I felt. He reassured me. "No, it was them. All the ugly racism he had to face. They killed him."

"He didn't have to do it," he added. "He could have lived out his life as a popular congressman. But he took on

---

that I had been blind. This was a humbling realization. When he insisted (through Mitchell) that I accompany the new police superintendent to be sworn in, he was giving me a chance to discuss the police misconduct problem and establish a relationship. I missed the obvious. Months later he insisted (through Mitchell) that I go to a site of a public housing crisis. (The question was whether a Cabrini Green high rise should be torn down.) The decision was made before I got there, but once again I failed to act. I didn't even talk to tenant leaders.

This made me realize he had cause to be angry with me.

the challenge, and it cost him." Mitchell was right. But a wiser man than I would not have written such an angry article. I had not paid him the respect he deserved.

I felt a little less alone when I found out that veteran political writer Salim Muwakkil had planned a similar article for *In These Times*. Rivlin recounts that "The piece quoted well-known figures in the black community who criticized, if not Washington himself, then his administration. More than one promised to aim at Washington the kind of protests suffered by Byrne if Washington didn't get off the dime. It was one deadline that Muwakkil was relieved to have missed."[37]

After Grayson Mitchell delivered the news that Washington had fired us that day, saying he didn't need us any more, I asked him if the mayor had said why I had to go. "He said 'He has his own agenda'" Mitchell told me. There was a pause, then we both laughed. Our agenda had been good enough in bad times.

Washington was a chess player and read widely on politics. He carried out long-term strategies. He had learned to deal with all kinds of people, and his election showed his genius for relating to them all. Outside his government he had many brilliant longtime friends and many contacts. But within his government he wanted people devoted to his agenda alone. The down side of this strategy though was that

---

[37] Rivlin, "Fire on the Prairie," 402. My story was cited by the *Chicago Tribune* on the 25th anniversary of Washington's death as charging that he was a "failure" as mayor. I wrote an angry letter to the editor pointing out that I had not called him a failure, and considered him in fact to be the best mayor in my lifetime.

after his unexpected death, his government was not in a position to lead a transition. If he had lived longer, his plan to transfer power to a new generation of leaders, such as Tim Evans, Jesus "Chuy" Garcia, and David Orr, would probably have been successful.

A Second Coup

Washington's body lay in state in the rotunda at City Hall, and over two hundred thousand people filed by to pay their respects, many grief-stricken by the loss. The whole city seemed to be in shock, and there was deep mourning in the black community.

Four thousand attended his funeral at Christ Universal Temple, and thousands more stood outside. Tim Evans and Jesus "Chuy" Garcia gave eulogies. They were the two aldermen closest to the mayor, and the consensus was that Evans was his natural successor, as floor leader and political spokesperson for the coalition. He had the full support of all the true progressives including council president pro tem David Orr, Danny Davis, Bobby Rush, Helen Shiller and Dorothy Tillman.

Garcia, who Washington considered his most able political ally, gave a poetic tribute from the Latino people.

"You came to our community to help build the
spirit of unity,
Where others didn't care you dared.
To gain what was essential, you cultivated our potential.

You made us see in 1983;

You gained some more in 1984;

You came alive in 1985;

And now that you are gone, we the people vow to stay strong.

The unity of our coalition is a tribute to the Washington tradition.

Today in '87, we know that you're in heaven. Adios, amigo. Adios."

The audience gave him a standing ovation.

After the service, thousands more lined the streets as his body was driven to burial at Oakwood Cemetery. There was to be a City Council meeting the next day and "Wild Bill" Henry was announcing that Gene Sawyer had more than enough votes to be elected acting mayor. His supporters included twelve black aldermen, Henry claimed.

In fact Henry and William Beavers, another hard-core machine alderman, were at City Hall already plotting who should succeed Washington before he was declared dead at Northwestern Hospital. Later that same afternoon, three of the men Jane Byrne had originally pointed to as the "evil cabal" -- Ed Vrdolyak, Ed Burke and Charlie Swibel -- met downtown to plan a takeover. Swibel was the longtime head of the CHA and a powerful wheeler dealer.

Two days later Burke had a long meeting with Alderman Sawyer, and the terms of the deal were agreed upon. Sawyer had a core of support among the black regulars, led by Henry and Beavers, and that would split the

Washington block. Chairmanships would be reassigned back to the regulars. It was much like the coup that Vrdolyak had engineered when Washington first got elected.

Worried that Sawyer would change his mind, or lose his black support, some 24 white aldermen and their representatives met on the North Side to prepare a backup plan to elect one of their own if necessary. North Side alderman Dick Mell made an all-out effort to be that candidate, telling the media he only needed two more votes. But he dropped his campaign when he was shown that Sawyer had the signed commitments of eleven black aldermen.

Meanwhile, judging by an analysis in the Tribune, the Evans negotiators were ineffective. There were no strategists like Coffey, Mitchell or Montgomery left in government.

"Jacky Grimshaw, Washington's chief lobbyist and an Evans backer, called for a meeting of all fifty aldermen to discuss the succession, but the Sawyer camp refused to attend. The meeting was canceled," according to the Tribune analysis.

Press secretary Alton Miller showed no interest in the succession question. He announced he was leaving the day after Washington died. Miller wrote of the day after Washington's death in his memoir, *"Harold Washington, the Mayor, the Man"*:

"A number were at work at the political office, two blocks from City Hall. Presumably they were working on the question of mayoral succession, planning a course of action designed to elect Ald. Tim Evans at the next City Council meeting. I had been at enough of those meetings at the political office. I pictured Jacky Grimshaw and Vince Bakeman (from that office) fussing with Ernie Barefield, and shuddered for Tim Evans."[38]

Jesse Jackson flew in from the Middle East and tried to mediate. He called a meeting of black aldermen and discovered how committed Sawyer's backers were. He met late into the night at his home with four Latino aldermen. "By keeping the four Hispanics at his home until late Friday night, Jackson caused Ald. Jesus Garcia (22nd) to miss a meeting in his own ward office that he had called, presumably to sell Evans to several independent aldermen," the Tribune relates. Although Rivlin gives a spirited defense of Jackson's efforts to negotiate, the fact is he did not hold much sway with the aldermen, either machine or Washington loyalist. And he certainly would not have been Washington's choice.

After Washington's funeral, alderman Henry announced that Sawyer had the signed support of twelve black aldermen, and was assured a victory at the City Council meeting the next day.

It seemed all was lost for Evans. That night, at the memorial being held for Washington at the University of

---

[38] Miller, *The Mayor, The Man,* 345.

Illinois pavilion, Sun-Times columnist Vernon Jarrett labeled the Sawyer aldermen sellouts, and called for action. "Treat your black enemies the same as you do the Ku Klux Klan," he said, and prevent them from going over to Washington's enemies.

"Jarrett may have offered the most memorable speech," Rivlin relates, "but it was Conrad Worrill who set the night's tone. He called on every person there to show up at City Hall in protest. 'We've come too far, he said, to be sold out by those negroes pretending to be black.' Gutierrez followed Worrill to the podium. 'We will surround City Hall because it is ours.'"[39]

And surround City Hall they did that Tuesday evening, filling the council chambers and streaming out onto LaSalle Street where the crowd was estimated at five thousand people. They carried signs such as "Uncle Tom Sawyer" and waved dollar bills at Sawyer shouting "How much, Gene?"; outside on the street they chanted "Sawyer's in a Cadillac, driving for Vrdolyak."

Meanwhile Sawyer was wavering back and forth. "About a dozen Washington aldermen, including Sawyer, gathered in Tim Evans' office," Rivlin relates. "Sawyer told the group that no job was worth the bloodshed going on in the black community. 'We can work this out.'"

---

[39] Rivlin, *Fire on the Prairie,* 416.

Ed Burke demanded to be admitted to the meeting and convinced Sawyer that he owed it to his colleagues to inform them of his decision. Sawyer left with Burke.

"The next his former allies saw of Sawyer he was walking into the council surrounded by bodyguards, his new found allies in tow. Sawyer's allies smiled the smile of victors."

Chicagoans were glued to their TVs as the meeting, scheduled for 6 p.m., finally got underway at nine. David Orr as president pro tem chaired the meeting. He was a solid Washington backer, a lakefront reformer who supported Tim Evans. He delayed the inevitable as long as he could, recognizing fellow Evans backers who filibustered with lengthy speeches. Ald. Mell stood up on his desk, waving his arms to be recognized, jumping up and down like an angry child, to no avail. But finally, at 1:50 a.m., Orr recognized Edwin Eisendraft, a Sawyer supporter who nominated him to be acting mayor.

At that point, according to A.C. Nielsen, some 480,000 people were still tuned to the live TV coverage. At 4 a.m., the vote was finally taken.

Only six black aldermen voted for Sawyer. The last minute campaign had swung six black aldermen to Evans. Even Beavers switched his vote, saying his office had received hundreds of angry calls that day. But it was not enough. Sawyer was elected with 29 votes.

The Washington coalition had been split. The machine had regained control. Rivlin fittingly titled this last chapter "The Empire Strikes Back."

Chapter 7

The Later Campaigns

Losing the Mayor's Office

That spring a student exhibit at the Art Institute included a painting of Washington dressed in women's underwear. As soon as the exhibit opened there were protests, and the City Council, meeting that day, passed resolutions condemning the painting.

After the meeting a group of black aldermen walked to the Art Institute and took down the painting. In the dispute that followed the police department took possession of the painting. The major media described the aldermen as buffoons, and many liberals condemned the action as a violation of free speech. The American Civil Liberties Union filed suit, and the city had to pay damages.

But couldn't white Chicago see how that painting was rubbing salt in the wounds inflicted by the Vrdolyak forces? Accusing him of being a child molester, McClain of being a pimp, now this. It was a final insult to his memory. In this day and age it's not supposed to matter, but for the record Washington was a discreet, active "ladies' man" his entire adult life, following a brief teenage marriage. He had dated his fiancee, Mary Ella Smith, for decades and she was a close friend and ally. Everyone who worked with him has stories of seeing him charm an attractive woman.

Just weeks before Washington died he had announced his strong support for a "Dream Ticket" made up of Richard Daley, Carol Moseley Braun and Aurelia Pucinski in the coming 1988 elections. Washington had opposed State's Attorney Daley in the last race. Carol Moseley Braun was the liberal black state legislator from Hyde Park now running for Recorder of Deeds. Aurelia Pucinski, running for City Clerk, was the daughter of Roman Pucinski, the Northwest Side alderman who had been one of the mayor's bitter foes.

Washington was consolidating his power within the Democratic Party. But his sudden death changed the political landscape, and his endorsement of Daley became a problem to his followers.

A week before the March 1988 primary, Clarence McClain called. He was working for Vrdolyak (!). Would I come to work for the campaign for the following week? Vrdolyak was trying to win the Republican nomination for Clerk of the Cook County Circuit Courts with a last-minute write-in campaign.

Wait a minute. Clarence McClain, hounded by the Vrdolyak 29 as a vicious pimp and child-molester, was now working for Fast-Eddie?

And he wanted me, the guy who used to call Vrdolyak "V.D." in our press office, to go over to the dark side?

But I was desperate for money. He was offering me $1,000 for one week's work. I told him I'd get back to him the next day. I was recently remarried, had a two-year-old son in the hospital, and was fired as the editor of Illinois Legal Times the month before.

Needless to say it was a quiet operation. Some twelve staffers, working out of an anonymous West Loop office building, each in isolation. I never saw Vrdolyak. But I did prepare a press conference for him on public housing. And he did receive press coverage as he declared at Cabrini Green that the Local Advisory Councils should take over management and then ownership of the developments.

In a way I was speaking to the ghost of Harold, still smarting at his refusal to consider the idea. As for Vrdolyak, he apparently could see that keeping poor blacks in their own neighborhood was an idea that appealed to his white ethnic base. But it was also an idea that appealed to some black nationalists as a step towards community empowerment.

Carol Moseley-Braun, running on Washington's "dream ticket" hired me to handle her press for the November 9, 1988 general election. I did the routine work to publicize her events. She had won awards for her liberal voting record and was an attractive, forceful woman. She won election easily. In fact the whole "dream ticket" won.

Much to my relief, Pucinski defeated Vrdolyak 59 percent to 41. Richard Daley led the ticket as he was reelected for a third term as Cook County State's Attorney, and everyone knew he was planning to run for mayor the following year.

***

The vote to make Gene Sawyer acting mayor had spelled the end of the solid black vote that was the base of Washington's power. Sawyer served as acting mayor for a year and a half before special elections were held for the remainder of Washington's term, and during that time he was able to add some elements of the black-nationalist movement to his solid support from the machine aldermen.

So Tim Evans didn't get a chance to challenge Sawyer until the Democratic primary of 1989. The problem was State's Attorney Richard M. Daley was running in that primary, so if he ran he would split the black vote. Instead he ran in the general election as the candidate of the Harold Washington Party

Jesse Jackson was among those who pressured Evans to support Sawyer in the primary, but how could he support him against Daley and then run against him? Daley's well-funded campaign, with former Tribune reporter David Axelrod as media adviser, beat Sawyer handily in the primary, getting 56 per cent of the vote to Sawyer's 43.

Axelrod had gone from heading Washington's media team in 1987 to working for the opposition in 1989. A later profile of Axelrod in the Tribune put it this way:

"To the surprise of liberal reformers, Axelrod signed up with the 1989 Mayoral campaign of Richard M. Daley, The Boss. On the younger Daley's retainer ever since, he has been a trusted inner circle advisor."[40]

In the general election, Richard M. Daley faced Evans and Vrdolyak. Daley presented himself as a reformer, pledging to carry out Washington-type programs while keeping peace with the machine. I was hired by the Evans campaign to assist in the press office. Evans had put together a campaign that seemed logical. Washington's chief of staff Earnest Barefield was campaign manager. Alderman Bobby Rush, a Washington loyalist, was in charge of field operations, and veteran independent strategist Don Rose was in charge of media.

But none of them had been involved in the '83 election (beyond Rush winning his own ward), and the uninspired, defensive '87 election was not a good model. Barefield was a careful, competent bureaucrat but not a campaigner.

I asked Evans for a meeting; we had worked well together as Washington's spokesmen. He invited me to his beautiful Kenwood home for coffee one evening. Evans had a highly successful private practice in addition to being an

---

[40] *Chicago Tribune*, June 24, 2007.

alderman, and his living room was ornate. His wife served us coffee and I laid out my thoughts on how the campaign could be reorganized along the lines of Washington's '83 primary. We should be holding issue- oriented media events along with reform groups, as well as coordinating with the Task Force and Slim Coleman's group. He was polite and friendly, but not persuaded. No changes would be made.

I did some routine research and writing for the press office. Rose certainly had good press connections, because I was surprised to see some of my research used by a political columnist as if it were his own.

But Evans was not the charming man of the people that Washington was, and Daley had a huge financial advantage, as well as quite a bit of lakefront liberal support to go along with his support on the North and Southwest Sides.

Daley won again, getting 56 per cent to Evans' 40 percent, with Vrdolyak, running as a Republican, getting 4 percent. Daley went on to be elected five more times, breaking his father's record by being mayor for 22 years. Axelrod was his media adviser for all those campaigns, and no one came as close as Sawyer and Evans had for another 17 years. As for Vrdolyak, that humiliating defeat marked the end of his political career.

The Aftermath

After his victory Daley announced a "rainbow government" with whites, blacks, Latinos and Asians in his cabinet. He was supported by many respected liberals, like state senator Dawn Clark Netsch. He presented himself as a "political androgyny, part machine and part reform," according to Bill Grimshaw in his book *Bitter Fruit*. After a year in office, Grimshaw concludes, it became clear that the reform part was only a veneer. "The rhetoric of reform masks a number of moves that have recentralized and closed government in the machine tradition."[41]

During those years I helped some elected leaders from the Local Advisory Council at Cabrini Green try to establish management and cooperative ownership of their buildings. The westernmost high rise, on Burling Street, had been featured on "60 Minutes" when tenants took over control of the building's lobby from the gang bangers and became security guards for their building. Their tenant management corporation carried out a number of reforms, such as setting up laundry facilities on the second floor.

In 1990, Jack Kemp, President H.W. Bush's head of the Department of Housing and Urban Development, proposed that all public housing Local Advisory Council's be encouraged to take over management of their developments, with the promise that after three years of successful management they could take over ownership.

Margaret Thatcher's conservative government was in the process of selling off its public housing. But in that case individual units were being sold to individual tenants. Kemp

---

[41] Grimshaw, *Bitter Fruit,* 216.

was talking about collective ownership, in effect a cooperative.

There were some initial success stories. Tenants in two St. Louis developments took over ownership and began to invest in neighborhood projects. In Chicago, the Local Advisory Councils began to plan for dramatic improvements. It looked like our old dreams from the Tenants Action Council were coming true.

In a November 29, 1993 article for *In These Times* I quoted a tenant leader: "'We have been working with an architect to show some of the things we could accomplish,' says Ken Hayes, vice president of the proposed Cabrini Extension Resident Management Corporation. 'We will have trees, orchards, crops of corn,' he says. 'We will link the buildings with secondfloor corridors and high-tech transportation.'

"Others talk of rooftop restaurants with a view of Lake Michigan, cooperatively owned supermarkets, tourist boats on the Chicago River -- a prosperous African-American community in the heart of Chicago."

But in that same article, tenant leaders said they knew what they were up against. The 70 acres of land under Cabrini and Green was worth a fortune to developers; within easy walking distance of Lake Michigan and a booming downtown.

"When they find oil on the reservation they move the Indians," said Josephine Trotter, president of the overall Cabrini Green LAC. That proved to be prophetic.

The Burling building was the furthest along in selfmanagement, and tenant leaders there, led by the LAC president Cora Moore, gained a written agreement with CHA to take over ownership. But then opposition came from an unexpected source.

Back in 1966 a civil rights lawsuit had been filed against the CHA charging deliberate segregation against black tenants. The evidence was overwhelming and in 1969 the judge ruled for the tenants in the famous Gautreaux case. The lead attorney, Alexander Polikoff, argued that the problem was segregation and the solution was integration. New public housing must be built in white areas.[42]

Now, in 1993, he opposed the Burling building's ownership plans because it would remain all black. The judge agreed and tenant leaders like Cora Moore were furious. Polikoff was supposed to be representing the interests of the tenants. The dreams of tenant ownership faded.

---

[42] In his lawsuit Polikoff relied heavily on the Brown vs. Board of Education decision, which seems a very different kind of situation. He devotes only a single paragraph to the original complaint in his book *Waiting for Gautreaux* (2006). By 1969, when the court ruled there must be scattered-site public housing, black leaders such as Fred Hampton had no use for this kind of assimilation program. They were reading Malcolm X and Frantz Fanon. The Black Panther Party was the most popular civil rights organization in the black community in 1969, according to national surveys.

The Gardner Campaign

In 1995 Joe Gardner tried to put together the Washington coalition for the February 28th Democratic mayoral primary. Under Washington he had been head of the Department of Neighborhoods, then head of the administration's political arm, the Political Education Project, and finally he became deputy director of CHA. He asked me to be his press secretary, but I was working as a science writer at Northwestern University, and they would not let me take a leave of absence, so I could only help out after hours. I was able to help identify a volunteer who had been handling his press as a Daley agent, and he was fired.

Gardner had support from important segments of the old coalition, including now congressmen Bobby Rush and Danny Davis, as well as Jesse Jackson and his Operation PUSH. Conrad Worrill did what he could to reassemble the Task Force.

But Sen. Carol Mosely Braun endorsed Daley, and so did a hundred black ministers. Even Dempsey Travis, Washington's good friend, endorsed Daley. And Daley refused to debate.

With a week to go I arranged a press conference at City Hall where Gardner supported an ordinance to limit the size and display of "For Sale" signs. He said it was to curb the practice of panic peddling. Crowded behind him were representatives from the "Save Our Neighborhood, Save Our City" coalition, representing the far Southwest and Northwest Sides. The City Hall reporters couldn't believe it.

So page three of the Sun-Times the next morning showed a smiling Gardner being cheered by a white crowd that many had considered racist. Nobody in the black community was worried about the size of for sale signs. We managed to get 32 per cent of the vote in the Democratic primary.

Gardner died of cancer the next year. A memorial service was held May 23rd at the Rockefeller Chapel at the University of Chicago, where a rainbow crowd of family, friends and activists paid their respects.

As we were leaving, Conrad Worrill and I saw each other and we embraced. We had done what we could for Joe's campaign, just as we had done for Harold's and Tim's.

Cabrini Comes Down

In 2000, the CHA announced a "Plan for Transformation" which called for tearing down all the public housing high rises and replacing them with new mixed-income housing. Once again it was Polikoff and the Gautreaux ruling that played the key role. Polikoff directed that the new mixed housing should be roughly one-third condominiums, one-third market rate, and one-third public housing.

The plan was roundly rejected by Cabrini tenants at a public hearing November 13th. I was at the back of the room, and at the tenants' leader's request I started the booing as

CHA director Vincent Lane announced his plan. The angry response was overwhelming.

But Lane insisted he was moving ahead anyway. His plan received some liberal support, but was it really wise to mix rich whites with a minority of poor blacks? It certainly didn't interest tenants, who wanted empowerment and community control.

But the plan was approved and all the city's public housing high rises were demolished, causing turmoil as tens of thousands of families were displaced. Cabrini had been a proud community of bowling clubs and church choirs and tumblers. Some of that spirit shines through in the movie "Cooley High," about the local high school. Many residents had risen to prominence, such as the current Cook County State's Attorney. Now residents were scattered, mostly to the poorest areas of the city, places that would accept their vouchers.

In theory the plan called for rehabbing all the low-rise housing and replacing the high-rise units with apartments in mixed-income buildings. In practice the CHA rehabilitated a few apartments, and then changed its mind. For instance at the Cabrini row houses they rehabbed 144 apartments, then left boarded up and vacant the remaining 442 units.

And as for the new mixed-income housing, it has gotten off to a very slow and difficult start. Only a handful of developments have been built, presumably because condo buyers are reluctant to buy in buildings with public housing. In the few that have been built, the tenants are treated like second-class citizens, as shown in the recent prize-winning film "70 Acres in Chicago: Cabrini Green."

The minority of public housing residents cannot vote on important matters. They must be drug tested and recertified each year, and many live in fear of eviction. There is virtually no interaction with the white condo owners. The documentary traces the whole sordid history of broken promises, and the sad remains of a once proud community.

So why did things go so wrong? Why did a well-intentioned lawsuit end up causing so much harm to the winning tenants? The answer lies in the original diagnosis of the problem. Yes black tenants were deliberately segregated. But they were also systematically discriminated against.

-- The giant concrete towers had no laundry facilities and no stores and no common areas. The vacant spaces around them increased isolation.

-- They were systematically cheated of basic services by corrupt companies and unions, as Renault Robinson discovered as head of CHA.

-- Federal welfare incentives led to whole developments with virtually no full-grown men, and surprise inspections to make sure.

-- They were preyed on by corrupt police units who controlled the drug traffic, as detailed in "Code of Silence," a report published by the Intercept and the Invisible Institute of Chicago.

-- Now the lawsuit that was supposed to represent them is determined to eliminate as much of their housing as it can.

****

The Gautreaux lawyers have sided with CHA and the developers at every turn. Lathrop Homes, a complex of apartments located along the Chicago River on the North Side, will lose some 525 units under the recently approved development plan, much to the dismay of longtime residents who had hoped the original 925 units would be restored.

On the Far-South Side, the isolated all-black Altgeld Gardens development is not the site of mixed-income buildings and condo buyers, but the Gautreaux lawyers are intent on reducing the population. While dangling the promise of a new library, the CHA has torn down 214 units, and is intent on demolishing 244 more, but they still face a battle with residents. Long time tenant leader Cheryl Johnson, now head of "People for Community Recovery," says historical landmark status may help their chances of fighting off the bulldozers. But she is absolutely perplexed that the case, whose lead plaintiff was from Altgeld, has turned out to be an enemy of the tenants. She wishes her group had the funds to challenge the Gautreaux lawyers.

Cabrini's Carol Steele thinks the Gautreaux lawyers have lost touch with reality. She doesn't think integration has anything to do with it. "Dorothy Gautreaux wanted to be closer to a hospital," she said. "How did it ever come to this?"

The Garcia Campaign

In 2015, Jesus "Chuy" Garcia challenged incumbent mayor Rahm Emanuel in the non-partisan April 17th primary election. He managed to force a run-off, and he received 34 per cent of the vote to Emanuel's 46 per cent. In the general election Garcia lost to Emanuel, but he did receive 44.3 per cent of the vote.

Garcia tried very hard to reassemble the Washington coalition. He had the support of County Clerk David Orr and most of the key elements from the Latino and progressive white communities. Emanuel had raised anger in the black community by closing 50 public schools at once, mostly in minority areas. But he had a giant campaign fund and received an endorsement from President Barack Obama, for whom he had served as chief of staff.

Garcia said the first person he called when he decided to run was Conrad Worrill, who had played such a key role in the 1983 election. Also supporting Emanuel were Congressman Bobby Rush and former alderman Dorothy Tillman, both former pillars of the Washington coalition. That coalition was shattered. Emanuel won the black vote handily. Of course a main factor was Obama's endorsement.[43]

Garcia did not run the strongest possible campaign. His first and only ad for most of the campaign had him calling for the hiring of 1,000 new police officers, as Emanuel had promised to do when he first ran. It was a reasonable position--Chicago police were severely understaffed--and Garcia emphasized that the new police would be trained in ways to cooperate with the community. But it was not an important issue for white progressives or for much of the black community.

As you might expect, I tried to talk Garcia into a press event at Cabrini where he could announce his support for the tenants who were demanding full rehabilitation of the 442 boarded up row houses. Tenant leaders such as LAC president Carol Steele were demanding the CHA fulfill its promise to rehab them all, the Gautreaux decision be damned.

Garcia went to the Cabrini row houses and met with tenant leaders but did not announce a position, and his visit received no press coverage. But in the final weeks he came on strong, winning the first two candidate debates and receiving powerful new union-backed commercials. He closed the gap, but his lack of support in the black community was fatal. But still he gained 44 per cent of the

---

[43] Obama was a community organizer in Chicago from 1985 to 1989 and was neutral about Council Wars. He was indifferent on the night Swayer was selected over Evans (see page 288 of *Dreams from My Father*).

vote, the best showing for an opponent of the Democratic machine since Harold.

The following year Garcia headed up Senator Bernie Sanders' campaign in Illinois and became a national spokesman to the Latino community. His call for an additional 1,000 police officers proved prophetic when Mayor Rahm Emanuel announced the urgent need for 1,000 more Chicago policemen.

Chapter 8

Harold's Legacy

Harold Washington had a profound effect on the city of Chicago. Whether Chicagoans voted for him or not, almost everyone came to like him and respect him. His prophesy in his inaugural address had been fulfilled.

"I hope someday to be remembered by history as the mayor who cared about people and was above all fair, a mayor who helped to heal our wounds, who stood the watch while the city and its people answered the greatest challenge in more than a century -- and who saw that city renewed."

Everyone saw that city services like garbage pickup and street paving were now equal in all neighborhoods. Many could see he had stood up to a corrupt regime and won the battle. His way with words and his sometimes theatrical acts, like dancing with Polish matrons on the Northwest side, or doing a jig on an imaginary grave of patronage on the lakefront, showed an impish good humor. His years as mayor substantially improved race relations in the city.

Yes, many of us were critical of his administration in 1987, and his bureaucratic government did stumble in addressing problems in areas such as public health and education. But he had only been able to truly govern for a little over a year, and many of us were unaware of some of the fundamental changes he had initiated, changes which have become more apparent over time.

For instance the set aside program for minorities that he began continues to this day, ensuring that at least 25 percent of city contracts go to minority businesses. Washington's set aside executive order was issued in 1985, and was codified as an ordinance in 1990 by Mayor Daley. It has been copied by many other cities and states across the country. It withstood a challenge in 2000 in a federal lawsuit against the city. City lawyers called Grayson Mitchell to ask about its origins, but Mitchell declined to tell them.

Washington's executive order allowing city employees to join unions was issued quietly in the early days of the administration, and when that was challenged in court, he and union leaders managed to push an ordinance through the deadlocked City Council and then to pass a state law for all public employees. This resulted in thousands of city employees becoming union members, and tens of thousands of government workers in Illinois. One union, the American Federation of State, County and Municipal Employees, now represents some 4,000 city workers and some 70,000 workers state wide. "If it weren't for Washington there probably still wouldn't be public employee unions in this state" said AFSCME Council 31 president Henry Bayer.

His executive order directing police to not turn people over to immigration authorities solely because they lacked documents, and other immigrant friendly measures, resulted in a large migration, especially from Mexico. The Latino population has more than doubled since 1983, and now stands at 30 per cent of the city, about the same as blacks and whites. This influx of families has enabled Chicago to maintain its population while many Midwest cities have shrunk.

Many of the other reforms live on, such as Zenobia Black's city wide homeless shelters, and Mike Holewinski's prevention of monopoly in the taxi industry. The work of Kari Moe and Rob Mier has resulted in much closer cooperation between city agencies and neighborhood organizations, and we still have our annual neighborhood festivals.

When Mayor Richard M. Daley succeeded him, he carried on some of Washington's initiatives, such as the set asides and neighborhood budget hearings, and giving neighborhood organizations city funds as "delegate agencies." Even one of Daley's signature accomplishments, the planting of trees in major streets, was foreshadowed by Washington's call for the city to plant a million trees.

But perhaps the most telling sign of Washington's ongoing influence is the presence of his loyalists in positions of authority today, 30 years later. Tim Evans, his floor leader and spokesman, is chief judge of the Cook County Courts. David Orr, his president pro tem, is County Clerk. Jesus "Chuy" Garcia, who he was grooming for higher office, challenged Mayor Rahm Emanuel in 2015, and remains a County Commissioner.

Current Chicago congressmen include Bobby Rush, Danny Davis and Luis Guittierez, all three solid Washington supporters 25 years ago. A fourth Chicago congressman, Jan Shakowski, helped Washington at a crucial time during the Epton campaign when she was with Illinois Public Action. Miguel del Valle, the first Latino elected to the state senate, served with distinction there for 20 years, and was City Clerk from 2006 to 2010. He ran for mayor in 2011. Kari Moe went on to become the longtime chief of staff for Sen. Paul Wellstone (Min), among the most progressive voices in Congress.[44]

Washington's opponents have not fared as well. Fred Roti, Bill Henry and William Beavers were all eventually indicted. Even Vrdolyak did ten months in federal prison and was recently indicted again. The biggest exception is Alderman Ed Burke, still chairman of the finance committee today, his law office still across the street. And until recently, William Beavers was a powerhouse in the Democratic machine.

***

---

[44] Helen Shiller served as aldermen for 24 years, and has now partnered with Jane Ramsey, longtime head of the Jewish Council on Urban Affairs, to form a progressive consulting agency. Slim Coleman has become a reverend and continues to be an activist. Zenobia Black went on to become executive director of the Charles A. Hayes Family Investment Center. Dorothy Tillman served as alderman for 20 years and led the fight for reparations for the black community. Richard Barnett continues to help elect progressives. Dick Simpson is professor of political science at the University of Illinois, Chicago. James Montgomery is a prominent attorney.

Washington was raised in a proud neighborhood by a political and religious father and a warm extended family. From an early age he was an avid reader and a determined competitor. He lived his whole life within the Democratic Party, convinced that this was his pathway to bring about more justice for his people.

Washington was a chess player and he made long-range plans. He went from state representative to state senator to congressman, each time painstakingly working the new sections of his base. He campaigned virtually every weekend, including frequent Sunday services.

He saw early on that a coalition of black and brown and a slice of white could gain power in Chicago, and established close ties with Latino activists who were also proud leaders of their people. During the campaign it was the fire of nationalism which made the difference.

When elected mayor he dutifully produced for all three parts of the coalition. For the black community, he named the first black police superintendent and the first black corporation counsel. He also established the unionization of city workers and set-asides to minority communities from city business. For the Latinos he was making Chicago a sanctuary city, the only one in the Midwest. He gave the white liberals freedom of information and careful spending. For all three, the fair and equal distribution of basic services.

Jesse Jackson ran twice for president on the momentum of his 1983 victory.

Washington was elected because of an uprising in the black community, but it took his leadership skills to bring victory. He demanded a voter registration drive as a condition for running, and that campaign registered 120,000 new voters, making the difference in the first elections. He won the bitter Epton campaign when he confronted the outrageous charges against him that Thursday night at Mundelein College. He steered the outrage over Vrdolyak's insults towards the upcoming committeemen races and won the showdown over city contracts. He vanquished Vrdolyak with the special aldermanic elections. He needed everything he had learned in a lifetime of politics to navigate to victory.

But for all his lifetime dedication to politics, Washington always made time for a night out on the town with old friends such as Bennett Johnson. Johnson says they never talked about government on those South Side jaunts.

Tribune columnist Clarence Page gives us a more poetic version of Washington's legacy in the beautiful book *Harold!: Photographs from the Washington Years*.

"Time helps one appreciate Harold Washington, not only the first black mayor of a city not always associated with brotherly love but also as a transformational leader with a prophetic vision and a perceptive wit. He was an insightful coalition-builder who broke away from the nation's most notorious big-city machine, challenged its dominance, and won. He did not live to lead his great American city into the new century, as he often hoped he would, but he prepared the way for those who do."

Epilogue

In February 2017 Aldermen Roderick Sawyer and Susan Sadlowski Garza announced a joint ordinance to require that all workers at Chicago airports be paid a "prevailing wage." A black-brown coalition?

Alderman Sawyer is the son of Mayor Eugene Sawyer, and leader of the City Council's Black Caucus. He has taken courageous stands against police misconduct. Garza, the newly elected alderman of Vrdolyak's 10th ward, is the daughter of long-time labor leader Ed Sadlowski of the Steelworker's Union.

They were joined by Ald. John Arena from the Northwest Side, a progressive who has made real improvements in his ward and the most outspoken critic of Mayor Emanuel at City Council meetings. Also Ald. Riccardo Munoz, from Garcia's Little Village, who was a major player in the original "prevailing wage" ordinance.

This group of black and brown and progressive white leaders shows the ongoing potential of the Washington coalition. His legacy lives on, with echoes of Fred Hampton and Martin Luther King.

Bibliography

Fire on the Prairie; Harold Washington, Chicago Politics and the roots of the Obama Presidency
By Gary Rivlin. Temple University Press, 2013.

Harold; the People's Mayor
By Dempsey Travis. Urban Research Press, 1988

Harold Washington; the Mayor, the Man
By Alton Miller. Bonus Books, 1989

Harold Washington; A Political Biography
By Florence Hamlish Levinsohn. Chicago Review Press, 1983

Harold! Photographs from the Washington Years
By Antonio Dicky, Marc PoKempner, Salim Muwakkil.
Northwestern University Press, 2007

Chicago Divided: The Making of a Black Mayor
By Paul Klepner. Northern Illinois University Press, 1985

Harold Washington and the Crises of Black Power in Chicago
By Abdul Alkalimat and Doug Gills, Twenty--First Century
Books,1989

Confronting the Color Line: The Broken Promise of the Civil Rights Movement in Chicago
By Alan Anderson and George Pickering. University of
Georgia Press, 1987

At Canaan's Edge; America in the King Years; 1965-68
By Taylor Branch. Simon & Schuster, 2007

JFK and the Unspeakable; Why he Died and why it Matters By James Douglass. Orbis Books, 2008

From the Bullet to the Ballot; The Illinois Chapter of the Black Panther Party and Racial Coalition Politics in Chicago
By Jakobi Williams. University of North Carolina Press, 2013

The Assassination of Fred Hampton; How the FBI and the Chicago Police Murdered a Black Panther
By Jeffrey Haas. Chicago Review Press, 2009

The Greatest: My Own Story
By Mohamed Ali and Richard Durham. Harper Collins, 1976

Bitter Fruit; Black Politics and the Chicago Machine. 1931-91
By William Grimshaw, University of Chicago Press, 1995

Dreams from My Father.
By Barack Obama, Three Rivers Press, 1995.

Troublemaker: A Memoir from the Front Lines of the Sixties
By Bill Zimmerman, Doubleday, 2011.

Author biography

Christopher Chandler began reporting at the City News Bureau in Chicago in 1963, and worked for five years at the Sun-Times and three years at WBBM-TV Channel 2. He has won a number of awards including First Place, Spot News in 1968 from the Illinois AP and an Emmy from the National Academy of Television Arts and Sciences in 1979.

He was a co-founder and associate editor of the Chicago Journalism Review, and editor of the Chicago Free Press, the Daily Planet, the New Patriot and North Avenue Magazine (NorthAvenueMagazine.net). He has written articles for the *New Republic*, *Chicago Magazine*, the *Reader*, *Streetwise* and *In These Times*.

He was Press Secretary during Harold Washington's primary campaign in 1983, and then Deputy Press Secretary during the general election campaign and the early years of the first Washington administration. He was later press secretary for U.S. Congressman Bobby Rush, and media director for the Government Accountability Project.

Acknowledgements

This book was made possible by help from Nora Willi, my collaborator, and my brother David, who brought it to life. I'd also like to thank my sons Chris and Bob for their support, and Timuel Black and Bob Starks for their valuable suggestions.